Mike McGr

JavaScript

Sixth edition

In easy steps is an imprint of In Easy Steps Limited
16 Hamilton Terrace · Holly Walk · Leamington Spa
Warwickshire · United Kingdom · CV32 4LY
www.ineasysteps.com

6th Edition

In Easy Steps Limited supports The Forest Stewardship Council (FSC),
the leading international forest certification organization. All our titles
that are printed on Greenpeace approved FSC certified paper carry the
FSC logo.

MIX
Paper from
responsible sources
FSC® C020837

Printed and bound in the United Kingdom

ISBN 978-1-84078-877-8

Contents

How to Use This Book

The examples in this book demonstrate JavaScript features that are supported by modern web browsers, and the screenshots illustrate the actual results produced by the listed code examples. Certain colorization conventions are used to clarify the code listed in the steps...

JavaScript code is colored blue, programmer-specified names are colored red, literal text is colored black, and code comments are colored green:

```
let sum = ( 9 + 12 ) / 3   // Equivalent to 21 / 3.
document.getElementById( 'info' ).innerHTML += 'Grouped sum: ' + sum
```

HTML tags are colored blue, literal text is colored black, and element attribute values are colored orange in both HTML and JavaScript code:

```
<p id="info">JavaScript in easy steps</p>
```

Additionally, in order to identify each source code file described in the steps, a file icon and file name appears in the margin alongside the steps:

page.html

external.js

data.json

data.xml

echo.pl

banner.svg

The source code of HTML documents used in the book's examples is not listed in full to avoid unnecessary repetition, but the listed HTML code is the entire fragment of the document to which the listed JavaScript code is applied. You can download a single ZIP archive file containing all the complete example files by following these easy steps:

1. Browse to **www.ineasysteps.com** then navigate to Free Resources and choose the Downloads section

2. Next, find JavaScript in easy steps, 6th edition in the list, then click on the hyperlink entitled All Code Examples to download the ZIP archive file

3. Now, extract the archive contents to any convenient location on your computer

If you don't achieve the result illustrated in any example, simply compare your code to that in the original example files you have downloaded to discover where you went wrong.

1 Get Started in JavaScript

This chapter is an introduction to the exciting world of JavaScript. It demonstrates how to add scripts to HTML documents that provide JavaScript variables and functions.

Meet JS

JavaScript ("JS") is an object-based scripting language whose interpreter is embedded inside web browser software such as Google Chrome, Microsoft Edge, Firefox, Opera, and Safari. This allows scripts contained in a web page to be interpreted when the page is loaded in the browser to provide functionality. For security reasons, JavaScript cannot read or write files, with the exception of "cookie" files that store minimal data.

Created by Brendan Eich at Netscape, JavaScript was first introduced in December 1995, and was initially named "LiveScript". It was soon renamed, however, to perhaps capitalize on the popularity of Sun Microsystem's Java programming language – although it bears little resemblance.

Before the introduction of JavaScript, web page functionality required the browser to call upon "server-side" scripts, resident on the web server, where slow response could impede performance. Calling upon "client-side" scripts resident on the user's system, overcame the latency problem and provided a superior experience.

JavaScript quickly became very popular but a disagreement arose between Netscape and Microsoft over its licensing – so Microsoft introduced its own version named "JScript". Although similar to JavaScript, the new JScript version had some extended features. Recognizing the danger of fragmentation, the JavaScript language was standardized by the Ecma International standards organization in June 1997 as "ECMAScript". This helped to stabilize core features but the name, sounding like some kind of skin disease, is not widely used and most people will always call the language "JavaScript".

Brendan Eich, creator of the JavaScript language, also co-founded the Mozilla project and helped launch the Firefox web browser.

The JavaScript examples in this book describe three key ingredients:

- **Language basics** – illustrating the mechanics of the language syntax, keywords, operators, structure, and built-in objects.

- **Web page functionality** – illustrating how to use the browser's Document Object Model (DOM) to provide user interaction.

- **Web applications** – illustrating responsive web-based apps and JavaScript Object Notation (JSON) techniques.

Include Scripts

To include JavaScript code directly in an HTML document it must be inserted between **\<script\>** and **\</script\>** tags, like this:

```
<script>
document.getElementById( 'message' ).innerText = 'Hello World!'
</script>
```

An HTML document can include multiple scripts, and these may be placed in the head or body section of the document. It is, however, recommended that you place scripts at the end of the body section (immediately before the **\</body\>** closing tag) so the browser can render the web page before interpreting the script.

JavaScript code can also be written in external plain text files that are given a **.js** file extension. This allows several different web pages to call upon the same script. In order to include an external script in the HTML document, the file name of the script must be assigned to a **src** attribute of the **\<script\>** tag, like this:

```
<script src="external_script.js"> </script>
```

Again, this can be placed in the head or body section of the document, and the browser will treat the script as though it was written directly at that position in the HTML document.

Assigning only the file name of an external script to the **src** attribute of a **\<script\>** tag requires the script file to be located in the same folder (directory) as the HTML document. If the script is located in an adjacent folder you can assign the relative path address of the file instead, like this:

```
<script src="js/external_script.js"> </script>
```

If the script is located elsewhere, you can assign the absolute path address of the file, like this:

```
<script src="https://www.example.com/js/external_script.js">
</script>
```

You can also specify content that will only appear in the web page if the user has disabled JavaScript in their web browser by including a **\<noscript\>** element in the body of the HTML document, like this:

```
<noscript>JavaScript is Not Enabled!</noscript>
```

Hot tip

You may see a **type="text/javascript"** attribute in a **\<script\>** tag but this is no longer required as JavaScript is now the default scripting language for HTML.

Beware

Do not include **\<script\>** and **\</script\>** tags in an external JavaScript file, only the script code.

Don't forget

External script files can make code maintenance easier but almost all examples in this book are standalone for clarity, so include the script code between tags directly in the HTML document.

Console Output

JavaScript can display output by dynamically writing content into an HTML element. For example, with this code:

document.getElementById('message').innerText = 'Hello World!'

The element is identified by the value assigned to its **id** attribute and the **innerText** property specifies text to be written there.

Hello World!

Additionally, JavaScript can display output by writing content into a pop-up dialog box, like this:

window.alert('Hello World!')

This calls the **alert( )** method of the **window** object to display the content specified within the ( ) parentheses in a dialog box.

This page says
Hello World!

OK

When developing in JavaScript, and learning the language, it is initially better to display output in the browser's JavaScript console, like this:

console.log('Hello World!')

This calls the **log( )** method of the **console** object to display the content specified within the ( ) parentheses in a console window. All leading browsers have a JavaScript console within their Developers Tools feature – typically accessed by pressing the F12 keyboard key. As the Google Chrome web browser is statistically the most popular browser at the time of writing it is used throughout this book to demonstrate JavaScript, and initially its console window is used to display output.

1 Create an HTML document that includes an empty paragraph and a script to display output in three ways

```
<p id="message"></p>
<script>
document.getElementById( 'message' ).innerText =
                                  'Hello World!'
window.alert( 'Hello World!' )
console.log( 'Hello World!' )
</script>
```

output.html

2 Save the HTML document then open it in your browser to see the output written in the paragraph and displayed in a dialog box – as illustrated opposite

3 Next, hit the **F12** key, or use your browser's menu to open its Developers Tools feature

4 Now, select the **Console** tab to see the output written into the console window

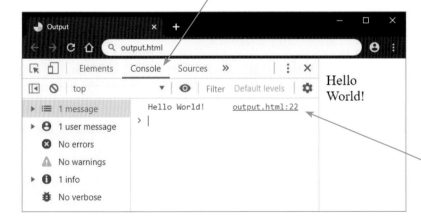

See that the console displays the output plus the name of the HTML document and the line number upon which the JavaScript code appears that created the output.

11

5 Click the ⬚ **Show/Hide** button to hide or show the sidebar, click the ⋮ **Customize** button to choose how the console window docks in the browser window, then click the ⊘ **Clear** button to clear all content from the console

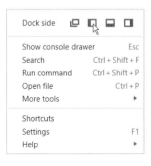

The JavaScript keywords are described on pages 14-15 and you will learn about operators, values, and expressions later.

Don't forget

An "expression" produces a value, whereas a "statement" performs an action.

Beware

Use the space bar to indent statements, as tab spacing may be treated differently when viewing the code in text editors.

Make Statements

JavaScript code is composed of a series of instructions called "statements", which are generally executed in top-to-bottom order as the browser's JavaScript engine proceeds through the script.

Each statement may contain any of the following components:

● **Keywords** – words that have special significance in the JavaScript language.

● **Operators** – special characters that perform an operation on one or more operands.

● **Values** – text strings, numbers, Boolean **true** or **false**, **undefined**, and **null**.

● **Expressions** – units of code that produce a single value.

In earlier JavaScript code each statement had to be terminated by a ; semicolon character – just as each sentence must end with a . period (full stop) character in the English language. This is now optional so may be omitted unless you wish to write multiple statements on a single line. In that case, the statements do need to be separated by a semicolon, like this:

statement ; statement ; statement

Some JavaScript programmers still prefer to end each statement with a semicolon. The examples in this book choose to omit them for the sake of concision but the choice is yours.

The JavaScript interpreter ignores tabs and spaces ("whitespace") so you should use spacing to make your code more readable. For example, when adding two numbers:

total = **100 + 200** rather than total=**100+200**

JavaScript statements are often grouped together within **{ }** curly brackets ("braces") in function blocks that can be repeatedly called to execute when required. It is good practice to indent those statements by two spaces to improve readability, like this:

```
{
  statement
  statement
  statement
}
```

The rules that govern the JavaScript language is called "syntax", and it recognizes two types of values – fixed and variable. Fixed numeric and text string values are called "literals":

- **Number literals** – whole number integers, such as **100**, or floating-point numbers such as **3.142**.

- **String literals** – text within either double quotes, such as **"JavaScript Fun"**, or single quotes such as **'JavaScript Fun'**.

Variable values are called, quite simply, "variables" and are used to store data within a script. They can be created using the JavaScript **let** keyword – for example, **let total** creates a variable named "total". The variable can be assigned a value to store using the JavaScript **=** assignment operator, like this:

let total = 300

Other JavaScript operators can be used to form expressions that will evaluate to a single value. Typically, an expression may be enclosed within **( )** parentheses like this expression that comprises numbers and the JavaScript **+** addition operator and evaluates to a single value of 100:

(80 + 20)

Expressions may also contain variable values too, like this expression that comprises the previous variable value, the JavaScript **-** subtraction operator, and a number, to also evaluate to a single value of 100:

(total - 200)

JavaScript is a case-sensitive language so variables named **total** and **Total** are regarded as two entirely different variables.

It is good practice to add explanatory comments to your JavaScript code to make it more easily understood by others, and by yourself when revisiting the code later. Anything that appears on a single line following **//** double slashes or between **/*** and ***/** character sequences on one or more lines will be ignored.

let total = 100   // This code WILL be executed.

```
/* let total = 100
   This code will NOT be executed. */
```

Hot tip

Decide on one form of quotes to use in your code for string literals and stick with it for consistency. The examples in this book use single quotes.

13

Hot tip

It is often useful to "comment-out" lines of code to prevent their execution when debugging code.

Avoid Keywords

In JavaScript code you can choose your own names for variables and functions. The names should be meaningful and reflect the purpose of the variable or function. Your names may comprise letters, numbers, and underscore characters, but they may not contain spaces or begin with a number. You must also avoid these words of special significance in the JavaScript language:

JavaScript Keywords			
abstract	arguments	await	boolean
break	byte	case	catch
char	class	const	continue
debugger	default	delete	do
double	else	enum	eval
export	extends	false	final
finally	float	for	function
goto	if	implements	import
in	instanceof	int	interface
let	long	native	new
null	package	private	protected
public	return	short	static
super	switch	synchronized	this
throw	throws	transient	true
try	typeof	var	void
volatile	while	with	yield

JavaScript Objects, Properties, and Methods			
Array	Date	eval	function
hasOwnProperty	Infinity	isFinite	isNaN
isPrototypeOf	length	Math	NaN
name	Number	Object	prototype
String	toString	undefined	valueOf

HTML Names, Window Objects, and Properties

alert	all	anchor	anchors
area	assign	blur	button
checkbox	clearInterval	clearTimeout	clientInformation
close	closed	confirm	constructor
crypto	decodeURI	decodeURIcomponent	defaultStatus
document	element	elements	embed
embeds	encodeURI	encodeURIcomponent	escape
event	fileUpload	focus	form
forms	frame	innerHeight	innerWidth
layer	layers	link	location
mimeTypes	navigate	navigator	frames
frameRate	hidden	history	image
images	offscreenBuffering	open	opener
option	outerHeight	outerWidth	packages
pageXOffset	pageYOffset	parent	parseFloat
parseInt	password	pkcs11	plugin
prompt	propertyIsEnum	radio	reset
screenX	screenY	scroll	secure
select	self	setInterval	setTimeout
status	submit	taint	text
textarea	top	unescape	untaint
window			

HTML Event Attributes
For Example:

onclick	ondblclick	onfocus	onfocusout
onkeydown	onkeypress	onkeyup	onload
onmousedown	onmouseup	onmouseover	onmouseout
onmousemove	onchange	onreset	onsubmit

Store Values

A "variable" is a container, common to every scripting and programming language, in which data can be stored and retrieved later. Unlike the "strongly typed" variables in most other languages, which must declare a particular data type they may contain, JavaScript variables are much easier to use because they are "loosely typed" – so they may contain any type of data:

Data Type	Example	Description
String	**'Hello World!'**	A string of text characters
Number	**3.142**	An integer or floating-point number
Boolean	**true**	A true (1) or false (0) value
Object	**console**	A user-defined or built-in object
Function	**log( )**	A user-defined function, a built-in function, or an object method
Symbol	**Symbol( )**	A unique property identifier
null	**null**	Absolutely nothing (not even zero)
undefined	**undefined**	A non-configured property

A variable name is an alias for the value it contains – using the name in script references its stored value.

Choose meaningful names for your variables to make the script easier to understand later.

A JavaScript variable can be declared using the **let**, **const**, or **var** keywords followed by a space and a name of your choosing. Variables declared with **let** can be reassigned new values as the script proceeds, whereas **const** (constant) does not allow this. The **var** keyword was used in JavaScript before the **let** keyword was introduced but is best avoided now as it does not prevent you declaring the same variable twice in the same context.

A **let** declaration of a variable in a script may simply create a variable to which a value can be assigned later, or may include an assignation to instantly "initialize" the variable with a value:

```
let myNumber                    // Declare a variable.
myNumber = 10                   // Initialize a variable.
let myString = 'Hello World!'   // Declare and initialize a variable.
```

Multiple variables may be declared on a single line too:

```
let i , j , k                   // Declare 3 variables.
let num =10 , char = 'C'        // Declare and initialize 2 variables.
```

Constant variables must, however, be initialized when declared:

```
const myName = 'Mike'
```

Upon initialization, JavaScript automatically sets the variable type for the value assigned. Subsequent assignation of a different data type later in the script can be made to change the variable type. The current variable type can be revealed by the **typeof** keyword.

1 Create an HTML document with a script that declares several variables that are assigned different data types
```
const firstName = 'Mike'
const valueOfPi = 3.142
let isValid = true
let jsObject = console
let jsMethod = console.log
let jsSymbol = Symbol( )
let emptyVariable = null
let unusedVariable
```

variables.html

2 Add statements to output the data type of each variable
```
console.log( 'firstName: ' + typeof firstName )
console.log( 'valueOfPi: ' + typeof valueOfPi )
console.log( 'isValid: ' + typeof isValid )
console.log( 'jsObject: ' + typeof jsObject )
console.log( 'jsMethod: ' + typeof jsMethod )
console.log( 'jsSymbol: ' + typeof jsSymbol )
console.log( 'emptyVariable: ' + typeof emptyVariable )
console.log( 'unusedVariable: ' + typeof unusedVariable )
```

The concatenation + operator is used here to output a combined text string.

3 Save the HTML document then open it in your browser and launch the console to see the data types in output

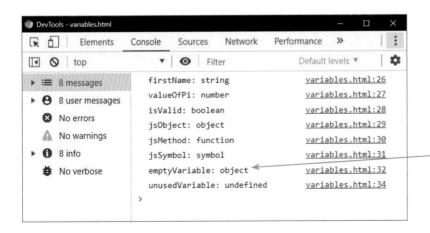

You should be surprised to see that the variable assigned a **null** value is described as being an **object** type, rather than a **null** type. This is a known error in the JavaScript language.

17

Create Functions

A function expression is simply one, or more, statements that are grouped together in **{ }** curly brackets for execution, and it returns a final single value. Functions may be called as required by a script to execute their statements. Those functions that belong to an object, such as **console.log( )**, are known as "methods" – to differentiate them from built-in and user-defined functions. Both have trailing parentheses that may accept "argument" values to be passed to the function for manipulation – for example, an argument passed in the parentheses of the **console.log( )** method.

The number of arguments passed to a function must normally match the number of "parameters" specified within the parentheses of the function block declaration. For example, a user-defined function requiring exactly one argument looks like this:

```
function function-name ( parameter ) {
  // Statements to be executed go here.
}
```

Multiple parameters can be specified as a comma-separated list and you can, optionally, specify a default value to be used when the function call does not pass an argument, like this:

```
function function-name ( parameter , parameter = value ) {
  // Statements to be executed go here.
}
```

You choose your own parameter names following the same naming conventions as for variable names. The parameter names can then be used within the function to reference the argument values passed from the parentheses of the function call.

A function block can include a **return** statement so that script flow continues at the caller – no further statements in the function get executed. It is typical to finally return the result of manipulating passed argument values back to the caller:

```
function function-name ( parameter , parameter ) {
  // Statements to be executed go here.

  return result
}
```

It is common for statements within a function block to include calls to other functions – to modularize scripts into blocks.

Hot tip

Notice that the preferred format of a function declaration places the **{** opening curly bracket on the same line as the **function** keyword.

Hot tip

You can omit the return statement, or use the **return** keyword without specifying a value, and the function will simply return an **undefined** value to the caller.

...cont'd

① Create an HTML document with a script that declares a function to return the squared value of a passed argument

```
function square ( arg ) {
  return arg * arg
}
```

functions.html

② Next, add a function that returns the result of an addition

```
function add ( argOne, argTwo = 10 ) {
  return argOne + argTwo
}
```

③ Now, add a function that returns the result of squaring and an addition by calling each of the functions above

```
function squareAdd ( arg ) {
  let result = square( arg )
  return result + add( arg )
}
```

④ Finally, add statements that call the functions and print the returned values in output strings

```
console.log( '8 x 8: ' + square( 8 ) )
console.log( '8 + 20: ' + add( 8, 20 ) )
console.log( '8 + 10: ' + add( 8 ) )
console.log( '(8 x 8) + (8 + 10): ' + squareAdd( 8 ) )
```

Notice that the default second parameter value (10) is used here when only one argument value is passed by the caller.

⑤ Save the HTML document, then open it in your browser and launch the console to see values returned from functions

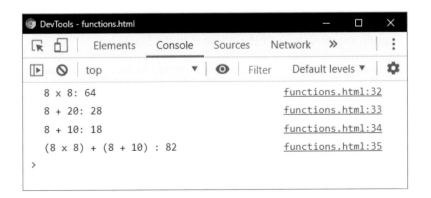

The * asterisk character is the arithmetical multiplication operator in JavaScript.

Assign Functions

Functions are really useful in JavaScript as they can be called ("invoked") to execute their statements whenever required, and the caller can pass different arguments to return different results.

It is important to recognize that the JavaScript ( ) parentheses operator is the component of the call statement that actually calls the function. This means a statement can assign a function to a variable by specifying just the function name. The variable can then be used to call the function in a statement that specifies the variable name followed by the ( ) operator. But beware, if you attempt to assign a function to a variable by specifying the function name followed by ( ) the function will be invoked and the value returned by that function will be assigned.

Function Hoisting

Although scripts are read by the JavaScript interpreter in top-to-bottom order it actually makes two sweeps. The first sweep looks for function declarations and remembers any it finds in a process known as "hoisting". The second sweep is when the script is actually executed by the interpreter. Hoisting allows function calls to appear in the script before the function declaration, as the interpreter has already recognized the function on the first sweep. The first sweep does not, however, recognize functions that have been assigned to variables using the **let** or **const** keywords!

Anonymous Functions

When assigning a function to a variable, a function name can be omitted as the function can be called in a statement specifying the variable name and the ( ) operator. These are called anonymous function expressions, and their syntax looks like this:

let *variable* = **function** (*parameters*) { *statements* ; **return** *value* }

Anonymous function expressions can also be made "self-invoking" by enclosing the entire function within ( ) parentheses and adding the ( ) parentheses operator at the end of the expression. This means that their statements are automatically executed one time when the script is first loaded by the browser. The syntax of a self-invoking function expression looks like this:

(**function** ( ) { *statements* ; **return** *value* }) ( )

Self-invoking functions are used widely throughout this book to execute example code when the script gets loaded.

1 Create an HTML document with a script that calls a function that has not yet been declared

```
console.log( 'Hoisted: ' + add( 100, 200 ) )
```

anonymous.html

2 Next, add below the function that is called above

```
function add( numOne, numTwo ) {
  return numOne + numTwo
}
```

3 Now, add a function that assigns the function above to a variable, then calls the assigned function

```
let addition = add
console.log( 'Assigned: ' + addition( 32, 64 ) )
```

4 Then, assign a similar, but anonymous, function to a variable and call that assigned function

```
let anon = function ( numOne, numTwo ) {
  let result = numOne + numTwo ; return result
}
console.log( 'Anonymous: ' + anon( 9, 1 ) )
```

Hot tip

5 Finally, assign the value returned from a self-invoking function to a variable and display that value

```
let iffy = ( function ( ) {
  let str = 'Self Invoked Output' ; return str
} ) ( )
console.log( iffy )
```

The significance of self-invoking functions may not be immediately obvious, but their importance should become clearer by the end of this chapter.

6 Save the HTML document, then open it in your browser and launch the console to see values returned from functions

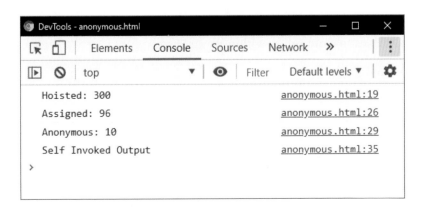

DevTools - anonymous.html

| Elements | Console | Sources | Network » |

top ▼ | ● Filter | Default levels ▼ ⚙

```
Hoisted: 300                    anonymous.html:19
Assigned: 96                    anonymous.html:26
Anonymous: 10                   anonymous.html:29
Self Invoked Output             anonymous.html:35
```

Recognize Scope

The extent to which variables are accessible in your scripts is determined by their "lexical scope" – the environment in which the variable was created. This can be either "global" or "local".

Global Scope

Variables created outside function blocks are accessible globally throughout the entire script. This means they exist continuously and are available to functions within the same script environment. At first glance this might seem very convenient, but it has a very serious drawback in that variables of the same name can conflict. For example, imagine that you have created a global **myName** variable that has been assigned your name, but then also include an external script in which another developer has created a global **myName** variable that has been assigned his or her name. Both like-named variables exist in the same script environment, so conflict. This is best avoided so you should not create global variables to store primitive values (all data types except Object and Function) within your scripts.

Local Scope

Variables created inside function blocks are accessible locally throughout the life of the function. They exist only while the function is executing, then they are destroyed. Their script environment is limited – from the point at which they are created, to the final **}** curly bracket, or the moment when the function returns. It is good practice to declare variables at the very beginning of the function block so their lexical scope is the duration of the function. This means that like-named variables can exist within separate functions without conflict. For example, a local **myName** variable can exist happily inside separate functions within your script and inside functions in included external scripts. It is recommended that you try to create only local variables to store values within your scripts.

Best Practice

Declaring global variables with the older **var** keyword allows like-named conflicting variables to overwrite their assigned values without warning. The more recent **let** and **const** keywords prohibit this and instead recognize the behavior as an "Uncaught SyntaxError". It is therefore recommended that you create variables declared using the **let** or **const** keywords to store values within your scripts.

Hot tip

You will discover how to catch errors on pages 60-61.

1 Create an external script that calls a function to output the value of a global variable

```
let myName = 'External Script'
function readName( ) { console.log( myName ) }
readName( )
```

external.js

2 Create an HTML document that includes the external script and adds a similar script

```
<script src="external.js"></script>
<script>
let myName = 'Internal Script'
function getName( ) { console.log( myName ) }
getName( )
</script>
```

scope.html

3 Save both files in the same folder, then open the HTML document to see a conflict error reported in the console

4 Edit both scripts to make the global variables into local variables then refresh the browser to see no conflict

```
function readName( ) {
  let myName = 'External Script' ; console.log( myName )
}
```

```
function getName( ) {
  let myName = 'Internal Script' ; console.log( myName )
}
```

Don't forget

The function calls **readName( )** and **getName( )** remain in the scripts without editing.

Use Closures

The previous example demonstrated the danger of creating global variables to store values in JavaScript, but sometimes you will want to store values that remain continuously accessible – for example, to remember an increasing score count as the script proceeds. How can you do this without using global variables to store primitive values? The answer lies with the use of "closures".

A closure is a function nested inside an outer function that retains access to variables declared in the outer function – because that is the lexical scope in which the nested function was created.

closure.html

1 Create an HTML document with a script that assigns a self-invoking anonymous function to a global variable
```
const add = ( function ( ) {
    // Statements to be inserted here.
} ) ( )
```

2 Next, insert statements to initialize a local variable and assign a function to a local variable in the same scope
```
let count = 0
const nested = function ( ) { return count = count + 1 }
```

3 Now, insert a statement to return the inner function – assigning the inner function to the global variable
```
return nested
```

4 Finally, add three identical function calls to the inner function that is now assigned to the global variable
```
console.log( 'Count is ' + add( ) )
console.log( 'Count is ' + add( ) )
console.log( 'Count is ' + add( ) )
```

5 Save the HTML document, then open it in your browser and launch the console to see values returned from a closure

Don't forget

Self-invoking function expressions are described on page 20. They execute their statements one time only. Here, you can use **console.log(add)** to confirm that the function expression has been assigned to the outer variable.

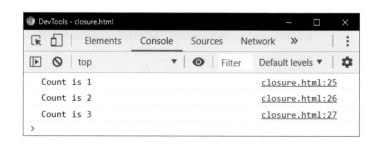

It can be difficult to grasp the concept of closures, as it would seem that the **count** variable in this example should be destroyed when the self-invoking function has completed execution. In order to better understand how closures work, you can explore the **prototype** property of the assigned function.

6 Add a statement at the end of the script to reveal how the assigned function has been constructed internally
console.log(add.prototype)

7 Save the HTML document, then refresh the browser and expand the "constructor" drop-down to see the scopes

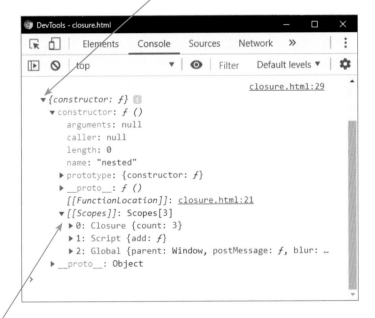

Closer inspection reveals that the assigned function has a special (Closure) scope in addition to the regular local (Script) scope and outer (Global) scope. This is how the **count** variable remains accessible via the assigned function yet, importantly, cannot be referenced in any other way.

The use of closures to hide persistent variables from other parts of your script is an important concept. It is similar to how "private" variables can be hidden in other programming languages and are only accessible via "getter" methods.

Hot tip

All JavaScript objects inherit properties and methods from a **prototype**. Standard JavaScript objects, such as functions, call an internal constructor function to create the object by defining its components.

Hot tip

Don't worry if you can't immediately understand how closures work. They can seem mystical at first, but will become clearer with experience. You can continue on and come back to this technique later.

Summary

- JavaScript code can be included in an HTML document directly or from an external file using **<script> </script>** tags.

- JavaScript can display output in an HTML element in an alert dialog box or in the browser's console window.

- JavaScript statements may contain keywords, operators, values, and expressions.

- The JavaScript interpreter ignores tabs and spaces.

- JavaScript statements can be grouped in **{ }** curly bracket function blocks that can be called to execute when required.

- Variable and function names may comprise letters, numbers, and underscore characters, but must avoid keywords.

- JavaScript variables may contain data types of String, Number, Boolean, Object, Function, Symbol, **null**, and **undefined**.

- Variables declared with the **let** keyword can be reassigned new values, but the **const** keyword does not allow this.

- A function expression has statements grouped in **{ }** curly brackets for execution, and it returns a final single value.

- The **( )** parentheses of a function expression may contain parameters for argument values to be passed from the caller.

- A function block can include a **return** statement to specify data to be passed back to the caller.

- The JavaScript **( )** parentheses operator calls the function.

- Hoisting allows function calls to appear in the script before the function declaration.

- Anonymous function expressions have no function name.

- Lexical scope is the environment in which the variable was created and can be global, local, or closure.

- Local variables should be used to store values, but global variables can be assigned functions to create closures.

- A closure is a function nested within an outer function that retains access to variables declared in the outer function.

2 Perform Useful Operations

This chapter describes the JavaScript operators and demonstrates how they can be used in your scripts.

Convert Values

Before performing operations in JavaScript it is important to recognize the data types of the values you are working with in order to avoid unexpected results. For example, the value **42** is a number, but the value **'42'** is a string, so attempting to perform an addition with **'42' + 8** will return a string result of **'428'**, not the number **50**. Happily, JavaScript provides a number of ways to return versions of values in other data types – without changing the value's original data type.

Strings to Numbers

The JavaScript **parseInt( )** built-in function can return an integer whole number version, in the number data type, of a string specified within its parentheses. For example, **parseInt('42')** will return the number **42**, so **42 + 8** will return a number result of **50**.

Similarly, the JavaScript **parseFloat( )** built-in function can return a floating-point number version, in the number data type, of a string specified within its parentheses.

Both these methods allow alphabetic characters to follow the numeric part of the specified string and strip them from the result – for example, **parseInt('42nd Street')** returns number **42**.

If either of these functions cannot find a numeric value at the beginning of the specified string, the result will be **NaN** – a JavaScript property meaning "Not a Number". You can also check if a value is not a number by specifying the value within the parentheses of a JavaScript **isNaN( )** built-in function. This, too, will first attempt to find a number at the beginning of the specified value and return **false** if it finds a number (even from a specified string), otherwise it will return **true** if it cannot find a number.

Numbers to Strings

The JavaScript **String( )** method can return a string representation, in the string data type, of a number specified within its parentheses – for example, **String(42)** will return the number **'42'** as a string data type.

Alternatively, you can append a **toString( )** method call onto a variable name to return a string representation of a stored number data type. For example, where a variable named "num" has been assigned a number, **num.toString( )** will return a string version of that stored number.

Hot tip

Conversion of data types is known as "coercion", and it can be explicit or implicit. Where '42' + 8 returns the string '428' this is implicit coercion. Where String(42) returns the string '42' this is explicit coercion.

1 Create an HTML document with a self-invoking anonymous function block that declares three variables
(**function ( ) {**

    let sum, net = '25', tax = 5.00

    // Statements to be inserted here.

}) ( )

conversion.html

2 Next, insert statements that create versions of different data types and print the result in an ouput string
```
sum = net + tax
console.log( 'sum: ' + sum + ' ' + typeof sum )

sum = parseFloat( net ) + tax
console.log( 'sum: ' + sum + ' ' + typeof sum )

console.log( 'tax: ' + tax + ' ' + typeof tax )
tax = tax.toString( )
console.log( 'tax: ' + tax + ' ' + typeof tax )

net = '$' + net
console.log( 'net: ' + net + ' ' + parseInt( net ) )
console.log( 'net Not a Number? ' + isNaN( net ) )
```

Don't forget

If you try **isNan(net)** before the '$' prefix is added to the string the result is **false** – because the method finds the number at the beginning of the '**25**' string.

29

3 Save the HTML document, then open it in your browser and launch the console to see the different versions

Do Arithmetic

The arithmetical operators commonly used in JavaScript are listed in the table below, together with the operation they perform:

Operator	Operation
+	Addition of numbers Concatenation of strings
–	Subtraction
*	Multiplication
/	Division
%	Modulus
++	Increment
– –	Decrement
**	Exponentiation

Hot tip

The ** exponentiation operator returns the result of a first operand raised to the power of a second operand.

Hot tip

An example using the modulus operator to determine odd or even numbers can be found on page 39.

Values specified in operation statements are called "operands". For example, in the statement **5 + 2** the + operator is supplied operand values of five and two. Notice that the + operator performs two kinds of operation depending on the type of operands. Numeric operands are added to return a sum total, but string operands are concatenated to return a single joined string.

The **%** modulus operator divides the first operand by the second operand and returns the remainder. Dividing by two will return either one or zero to usefully determine whether the first operand is an odd number or an even number.

The **++** increment operator and -- decrement operator alter the value of a single operand by one, and return the new value. These operators are most commonly used to count iterations of a loop and can be used in two different ways to subtly different effect. When placed before the operand (prefixed) its value is immediately changed before the expression is evaluated, but when placed after the operand (postfixed) the expression is evaluated first then the value gets changed.

...cont'd

1 Create an HTML document with a self-invoking anonymous function block
(function ( ) {

// Statements to be inserted here.

}) ( )

arithmetic.html

2 Next, insert statements that assign values to variables using each arithmetical operator and print each result in an output string
let sum = 80 + 20 ; console.log('Addition: ' + sum)

let sub = sum - 50 ; console.log('Subtraction: ' + sub)

let mul = sum * 5 ; console.log('Multiplication: ' + mul)

let div = sum / 4 ; console.log('Division: ' + div)

let mod = sum % 2 ; console.log('Modulus: ' + mod)

let inc = ++sum ; console.log('Increment: ' + inc)

let dec = --sum ; console.log('Decrement: ' + dec)

3 Save the HTML document, then open it in your browser and launch the console to see the arithmetic results

Assign Values

The operators that are commonly used in JavaScript to assign values are all listed in the table below. All except the simple = assignment operator are shorthand forms of longer expressions, so each equivalent is also given for clarity.

Operator	Example	Equivalent
=	a = b	a = b
+=	a += b	a = (a + b)
–=	a –= b	a = (a – b)
*=	a *= b	a = (a * b)
/=	a /= b	a = (a / b)
%=	a %= b	a = (a % b)
**=	a **= b	a = (a ** b)

It is important to think of the = operator as meaning "assign" rather than "equals" to avoid confusion with the JavaScript === equality operator.

In the = example in the table, the variable **a** gets assigned the value contained in variable **b** to become its new stored value.

The combined += operator is most useful and can be employed to append a string onto an existing string. For example, with a variable string **let str = 'JavaScript'** and **str += ' Fun'** the variable now stores the combined string **'JavaScript Fun'**.

Numerically speaking, the += example in the table will add the value contained in variable **a** to that contained in variable **b** then assign the sum total to become the new value stored in variable **a**.

All other combined assignment operators work in a similar way to the += operator. They each perform the arithmetical operation on their two operands first, then assign the result of that operation to the first variable – so that becomes its new stored value.

Hot tip

The === equality operator compares values and is fully explained on page 34.

1 Create an HTML document with a self-invoking anonymous function that concatenates two strings
(function ( ) {

```
let msg = 'JavaScript' ; msg += ' Fun'
console.log( 'Add & concatenate: ' +  msg )
```

// Statements to be inserted here.

}) ( )

assignment.html

2 Next, insert statements that use combined operators to perform arithmetic and assign results for output
```
let sum = 5.00 ; sum += 2.50
console.log( 'Add & assign decimal: ' +  sum )

sum = 8 ; sum -= 4
console.log( 'Subtract & assign integer: ' +  sum )

sum = 8 ; sum *= 4
console.log( 'Multiply & assign integer: ' +  sum )

sum = 8 ; sum /= 4
console.log( 'Divide & assign integer: ' +  sum )

sum = 8 ; sum %= 4
console.log( 'Modulus & assign integer: ' +  sum )
```

3 Save the HTML document, then open it in your browser and launch the console to see the assigned values

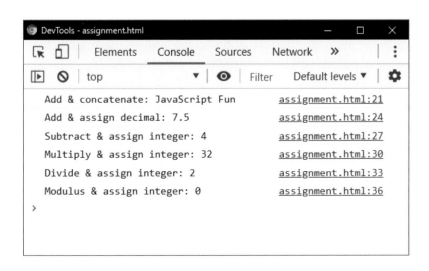

Make Comparisons

The operators that are commonly used in JavaScript to compare two values are all listed in the table below:

Operator	Comparison
===	Equality
!==	Inequality
>	Greater than
<	Less than
>=	Greater than or equal to
<=	Less than or equal to

Hot tip

An example using the < less than operator in a loop structure can be found on page 53.

Beware

There is also a == equality operator and a != inequality operator, but these may produce unexpected results as, unlike === and !==, they do not ensure the values being compared are of the same data type. This means that **25 == '25'** returns **true**, whereas **25 === '25'** returns **false**. Always use the three-character versions so your scripts will make accurate comparisons.

The === equality operator compares two operands and will return a Boolean **true** value if they are exactly equal, otherwise it will return a Boolean **false** value. If the operands are identical numbers they are equal; if the operands are strings containing the same characters in the same positions they are equal; if the operands are Boolean values that are both **true**, or both **false**, they are equal. Conversely, the !== inequality operator returns true if the two operands are not equal, using the same rules as the === equality operator.

Equality and inequality operators are useful in comparing two values to perform "conditional branching", where the script will follow a particular direction according to the result.

The > greater than operator compares two operands and returns **true** if the first is greater in value than the second. The < less than operator makes the same comparison but returns **true** when the first is less in value than the second. Adding the = character after the > greater than operator or the < less than operator makes them also return **true** when the two operands are equal.

The > greater than and < less than operators are frequently used to test the value of a counter variable in a loop structure.

...cont'd

1 Create an HTML document with a self-invoking anonymous function that declares three variables
(function ( ) {

   let comparison, sum = 8, str = 'JavaScript'

   // Statements to be inserted here.

}) ( )

comparison.html

2 Next, insert statements that use comparison operators to assign Boolean results for output
```
comparison = str === 'JAVASCRIPT'
console.log( 'String Equality? ' + comparison )

comparison = str === 'JavaScript'
console.log( 'String Equality? ' + comparison )

comparison = sum === 8
console.log( 'Number Equality? ' + comparison )

comparison = sum > 5
console.log( 'Greater Than? ' + comparison )

comparison = sum < 5
console.log( 'Less Than? ' + comparison )

comparison = sum <= 8
console.log( 'Less Than or Equal To? ' + comparison )
```

3 Save the HTML document, then open it in your browser and launch the console to see the assigned results

JavaScript is case-sensitive, so character capitalization must match for compared strings to be equal.

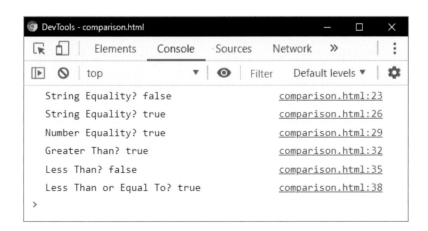

Assess Logic

The three logical operators that can be used in JavaScript are listed in the table below:

Operator	Operation
&&	Logical AND
||	Logical OR
!	Logical NOT

The logical operators are typically used with operands that have a Boolean value of **true** or **false** – or values that can convert to **true** or **false**.

The **&&** logical AND operator will evaluate two operands and return **true** only if both operands are themselves **true**. Otherwise, the **&&** AND operator will return **false**. This is often used in conditional branching where the direction of the script is determined by testing two conditions. If both conditions are satisfied, the script will follow a particular direction, otherwise it will follow a different direction.

Unlike the **&&** logical AND operator, which needs both operands to be **true**, the **||** logical OR operator will evaluate two operands and return **true** if either one of the operands is itself **true**. If neither operand is **true** then the **||** OR operator will return **false**. This is useful to have a script perform a certain action if either one of two test conditions is satisfied.

The third logical operator is the **!** logical NOT operator that is used before a single operand, and it returns the inverse value of the operand. For example, if variable named "tog" had a **true** value then **!tog** would return **false**. This is useful to "toggle" the value of a variable in successive loop iterations with a statement such as **tog = !a** so that the value is reversed on each iteration – like flicking a light switch on and off.

The term "Boolean" refers to a system of logical thought developed by the English mathematician George Boole (1815-1864).

...cont'd

1 Create an HTML document with a self-invoking anonymous function that declares three variables
(function ( ) {

> let result, yes = true, no = false

> // Statements to be inserted here.

}) ( )

logic.html

2 Next, insert statements that use logical operators to assign Boolean results for output
```
result = yes && yes
console.log( 'Are both true? ' + result )

result = yes && no
console.log( 'Are both still true? ' + result )

result = yes || no
console.log( 'Are either true? ' + result )

result = no || no
console.log( 'Are either still true? ' + result )

console.log( 'Original value: ' + yes )
yes = !yes
console.log( 'Toggled value: ' + yes )
```

3 Save the HTML document, then open it in your browser and launch the console to see the returned results

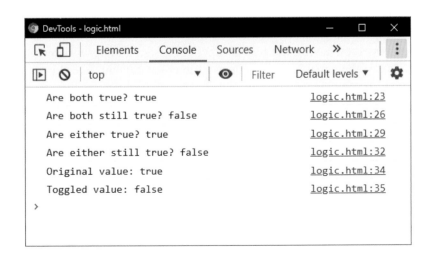

Hot tip

See that **false && false** returns **false**, not **true** – perhaps demonstrating the maxim "two wrongs don't make a right".

Examine Conditions

Possibly, the JavaScript author's favorite operator is the **?:** conditional operator. This operator is also known as the "ternary" operator – meaning composed of three parts.

The ternary operator evaluates a specified condition for a **true** or **false** value then executes one of two specified statements according to the result. Its syntax looks like this:

condition ? if-true-do-this : if-false-do-this

Where multiple actions are required to be performed, according to the result of the condition evaluation, each specified statement may be a function call to execute multiple statements in each function – for example, calling functions to execute multiple statements according to the Boolean value of a variable named "flag", like this:

flag === true ? doThis( ) : doThat( )

In this example, the **===** equality operator and **true** keyword are actually superfluous, as operators that evaluate an expression for a Boolean value automatically perform this assessment, so the example could be more simply stated as:

flag ? doThis( ) : doThat( )

Alternatively, the two statements specified to the ternary operator might assign a value to a variable according to the result of the condition evaluation, like this:

flag ? str = 'Go left' : str = 'Go right'

While this is syntactically correct, it can be more elegantly expressed by having the ternary operator assign an appropriate value to the variable in a single assignment statement, like this:

str = flag ? 'Go left' : 'Go right'

Where the condition evaluates the parity of a numeric value, the two statements can supply alternatives according to whether the evaluation determines the number to be even or odd.

Don't forget

The ternary operator has three operands – the one before the **?** and those either side of the **:** colon.

1 Create an HTML document with a self-invoking anonymous function that declares two variables

```
( function ( ) {

    const numOne = 8, numTwo = 3

    // Statements to be inserted here.

} ) ( )
```

ternary.html

2 Next, insert statements to output a string with appropriate grammar for quantity

```
let verb = ( numOne !== 1 ) ? ' are ' : ' is '
console.log( 'There' + verb + numOne )
```

3 Now, insert statements to ouput strings correctly describing the parity of two variable values

```
let parity = ( numOne % 2 !== 0 ) ? 'Odd' : 'Even'
console.log( numOne + ' is ' + parity )

parity = ( numTwo % 2 !== 0 ) ? 'Odd' : 'Even'
console.log( numTwo + ' is ' + parity )
```

4 Finally, insert statements to output a string reporting the greater of two variable values

```
let max = ( numOne > numTwo ) ? numOne : numTwo
console.log( max + ' is the Greater Number' )
```

5 Save the HTML document, then open it in your browser and launch the console to see the string descriptions

Hot tip

The ternary operator can return values of any data type – string, number, Boolean, etc.

Juggle Bits

JavaScript "bitwise" operators regard their operands as a sequence of 32 bits in which each bit may contain a value of zero (0) or one (1). Each bit contributes a decimal component only when that bit contains a one. Components are designated right-to-left from the "Least Significant Bit" (LSB) to the "Most Significant Bit" (MSB). The binary number in the eight-bit pattern below represents decimal 50 as denoted by the bits set with a **1** value (2 + 16 + 32 = 50).

Many JavaScript authors never use bitwise operators but it is useful to understand what they are and how they may be used.

Bit No.	8	7	6	5	4	3	2	1
Decimal	128	64	32	16	8	4	2	1
Binary	0	0	1	1	0	0	1	0

It is possible to manipulate individual bits of the sequence using the JavaScript bitwise operators listed in the table below.

A "byte" has 8 bits, and each half of a byte is known as a "nibble" (4 bits). The binary numbers in the examples in this table describe values stored in a nibble.

Operator	Name	Binary number operation:
|	OR	Return a **1** in each bit where either of two compared bits is a **1** Example: **1010 | 0101 = 1111**
&	AND	Return a **1** in each bit where both of two compared bits is a **1** Example: **1010 & 1100 = 1000**
~	NOT	Return a **1** in each bit where the bit is not **1**, and return **0** where the bit is **1** Example: **~ 1010 = 0101**
^	XOR	Return a **1** in each bit where only one of two compared bits is a **1** Example: **1010 ^ 0100 = 1110**
<<	Shift left	Push zeros in from the right, to move each bit a number of bits to the left Example: **0010 << 2 = 1000**
>>	Signed shift right	Push copies of the leftmost bit in from the left, to move each bit a number of bits to the right. Example: **1000 >> 2 = 0010**
>>>	Shift right	Push zeros in from the left, to move each bit a number of bits to the right Example: **1000 >> 2 = 0010**

1 Create an HTML document with a self-invoking anonymous function that declares two variables
(**function ( ) {**

    let numOne = 10, numTwo = 5

    // Statements to be inserted here.

}) ( )

bitwise.html

2 Next, insert statements to simply output strings that confirm the initial values stored in each variable
console.log('numOne: ' + numOne)
console.log('numTwo: ' + numTwo)

3 Now, insert statements to swap the values stored in each variable using bitwise operations
numOne = numOne ^ numTwo
        // 1010 ^ 0101 = 1111 = (decimal 15)
numTwo = numOne ^ numTwo
        // 1111 ^ 0101 = 1010 (decimal 10)
numOne = numOne ^ numTwo
        // 1111 ^ 1010 = 0101 (decimal 5)

Hot tip

Notice how this example uses the special \n escape sequence to create a line break in the console output.

4 Finally, insert statements to output a line break and strings to confirm the final values stored in each variable
console.log('\n' + 'numOne: ' + numOne)
console.log('numTwo: ' + numTwo)

5 Save the HTML document, then open it in your browser and launch the console to see the swapped values

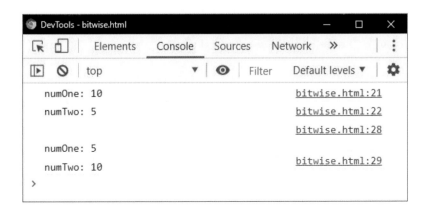

41

Force Order

JavaScript operators have different levels of priority to determine the order in which a statement containing multiple different operators gets evaluated – those with higher priority take precedence over those with lower priority. The table below lists each type of operator in order of highest to lowest priority from top to bottom of the table:

Priority

Hot tip

The [ ] operator is introduced in the section that demonstrates arrays beginning on page 70. Meanwhile, note that the . period (full stop) operator, used in dot notation such as **console.log( )**, is given high precedence for early recognition of the object and its member.

Operator	Operation
( )	Expression grouping
. [ ] ( )	Object Member Array Member Function Call
++ --	Postfix Increment, Postfix Decrement
++ -- ! ~	Prefix Increment, Prefix Decrement Logical NOT, Bitwise NOT
**	Exponentiation
* / %	Multiplication, Division, Modulus
+ –	Addition, Subtraction
<< >> >>>	Bitwise shift
< <= => >	Comparison
=== === !== !=	Equality, Inequality
&	Bitwise AND
^	Bitwise XOR
|	Bitwise OR
&&	Logical AND
||	Logical OR
?:	Ternary conditional
= += –= *= /= %= &= ^= |= <<= >>= >>>=	Assignment
,	Comma

42

1 Create an HTML document with a self-invoking anonymous function that initializes a variable with the result of an ungrouped expression and outputs its value
(function ( ) {

```
let sum = 9 + 12 / 3          // Equivalent to 9 + 4.
console.log( 'Ungrouped sum: ' + sum )
```

}) ( )

precedence.html

2 Save the HTML document, then open it in your browser and launch the console to see the resulting value

The evaluation first computes the division, as its operator has higher priority than the addition operator, so the result is 13. But you can force the order of precedence by grouping an expression within parentheses so it will be evaluated first, because the ( ) operator has the very highest priority of all operators.

3 Edit the statements within the function to force the order of evaluation so the addition is performed before division
```
let sum = ( 9 + 12 ) / 3          // Equivalent to 21 / 3.
console.log( 'Grouped sum: ' + sum )
```

4 Save the HTML document once more, then refresh your browser to see the new resulting value

Hot tip

Make a habit of using parentheses to group expressions and thereby set the precedence order of evaluation.

43

Summary

- **parseInt( )** and **parseFloat( )** can convert strings to numbers, but **String( )** and **toString( )** can convert numbers to strings.

- The **isNaN( )** function tests its argument for a **NaN** value.

- Arithmetic operators perform regular arithmetic plus **%** modulus, **++** increment, **--** decrement, and ****** exponentiation.

- When the **++** increment or **– –** decrement operator prefix the operand its value is changed immediately, but when they are postfixed after the operand the expression is evaluated first.

- The **=** operator can be combined with an arithmetic operator to perform an arithmetical operation then assign its result.

- The **+=** operator is useful to append to an existing string.

- Two operands can be compared for **===** equality, **!==** inequality, **>** greater than value, or **<** less than value.

- The **<=** and **>=** combined comparison operators also return **true** when both operands are equal.

- The logical **&&** AND operator evaluates two operands and returns **true** when both operands are **true**, but the logical **||** OR operator returns **true** when either operand is **true**.

- The logical **!** NOT operator can prefix a single operand to return its inverse value.

- Ternary operator **?:** evaluates a condition for **true** or **false** then executes one of two statements according to the result.

- JavaScript bitwise operators can manipulate individual bits of a binary sequence to perform binary arithmetic.

- JavaScript operators have different levels of priority to determine the order in which a statement gets evaluated.

- The order of precedence can be forced by grouping an expression within **( )** parentheses so it will be evaluated first.

3 Manage the Script Flow

Branch If

The progress of any script or computer program depends upon the evaluation of conditions to determine the direction of flow. Each evaluation may present one or more branches along which to continue according to the result of the evaluation.

In JavaScript, the basic conditional test is performed with the **if** keyword to test a condition for a Boolean **true** or **false** value. When the result is **true**, a statement following the evaluation will be executed, otherwise this is skipped and flow continues at the next subsequent statement.

The syntax of an **if** statement demands that the condition to be tested is placed within parentheses after the **if** keyword, and looks like this:

if (*condition*) *execute-this-statement-when-true*

An **if** statement may also specify multiple statements to be executed when the result is true by enclosing those statements within braces, like this:

```
if ( condition )
{
  execute-this-statement-when-true
  execute-this-statement-when-true
  execute-this-statement-when-true
}
```

The evaluation of a condition and the execution of actions according to its result simply reflects the real-life thought process – for example, the actions you might execute on a summer day:

```
let temperature = readThermometer( )
const tolerable = 25

if ( temperature > tolerable )
{
  turn_on_air-conditioning( )
  get_a_cool_drink( )
  stay_in_shade( )
}
```

The conditional test is equivalent to **if(*condition* === true)**, but as it automatically performs the equality test for a **true** value there is no need to include **=== true** in the parentheses.

Hot tip

It is recommended that you enclose even single statements to be executed within braces – to maintain a consistent coding style.

1 Create an HTML document with a self-invoking function that begins by initializing a Boolean variable
```
let flag = true
```

if.html

2 Next, insert statements to perform conditional tests of the variable's Boolean value
```
if( !flag )
{
  console.log( 'Power is OFF' )
}

if( flag )
{
  console.log( 'Power is ON' )
}
```

The logical **!** NOT operator is used here to invert the conditional test so it becomes equivalent to
if(flag === false)

3 Now, insert statements to perform conditional tests of an expression that compares two integers
```
if( 7 < 2 )
{
  console.log( 'Failure' )
}

if( 7 > 2 )
{
  console.log( 'Success' )
}
```

The script code that creates the function block is omitted from this example, and most further examples, to conserve page space. You can refer back to page 20 for instruction on how to create anonymous self-invoking functions.

4 Save the HTML document, then open it in your browser and launch the console to see which output statements get executed and which ones are ignored

Branch Alternatives

An **if** statement, which tests a condition for a Boolean value and only executes its statements when the result is **true,** provides a single branch that the script may follow. An alternative branch that the script can follow when the result is **false** can be provided by extending an **if** statement with the **else** keyword.

An **else** statement follows after the **if** statement, like this:

if (*condition*) *execute-this-statement-when-true*
else *execute-this-statement-when-false*

An **if else** statement may also specify multiple statements to be executed by enclosing those statements within braces, like this:

```
if ( condition )
{
  execute-this-statement-when-true
  execute-this-statement-when-true
}
else
{
  execute-this-statement-when-false
  execute-this-statement-when-false
}
```

Multiple branches can be provided by making subsequent conditional **if** tests at the start of each **else** statement block, like this:

```
if ( condition )
{
  execute-these-statements-when-true
}
else if ( condition )
{
  execute-these-statements-when-true
}
else if ( condition )
{
  execute-these-statements-when-true
}
else
{
  execute-these-statements-when-false
}
```

Hot tip

Once a condition is found to be **true** in an **if else** statement, its associated statements are executed, then flow continues after the **if else** statement – without evaluating subsequent **else** statements.

An **if else if** statement might repeatedly test a variable for a range of values or might test a variety of conditions. The final **else** statement acts as a default when no conditions are found to be **true.**

1 Create an HTML document with a self-invoking function that begins by initializing two variables

```
let flag = false
const num = 10
```

else.html

2 Next, insert statements to perform conditional tests of the first variable's Boolean value

```
if( !flag )
{
  console.log( 'Power is OFF' )
}
else
{
  console.log( 'Power is ON' )
}
```

3 Now, insert statements to perform conditional tests of the second variable's numeric value

```
if( num === 5 )
{
  console.log( 'Number is Five' )
}
else if( num === 10 )
{
  console.log( 'Number is Ten' )
}
else
{
  console.log( 'Number is Neither Five nor Ten' )
}
```

Don't forget

The **else** statement specifies an alternative when a conditional test is **false**, but an **else if** statement specifies a new conditional test.

49

4 Save the HTML document, then open it in your browser and launch the console to see which output statements get executed and which ones are ignored

Omission of the **break** statement allows the script to also execute statements associated with subsequent unmatching **case** values.

Switch Alternatives

Conditionally branching script flow using **if else** statements is fine for testing just a few conditions but can become unwieldy when there are a large number of conditions to test. In that situation it is often both more efficient and more elegant to use a **switch** statement rather than **if else** statements.

A **switch** statement works in an unusual way – it first evaluates a specified expression, then seeks a match for the resulting value. Where a match is found, the **switch** statement will execute one or more statements associated with that value, otherwise it will execute one or more statements specified as "default statements".

The **switch** statement begins by enclosing the expression to be evaluated within parentheses after the **switch** keyword. This is followed by a pair of **{ }** braces that contain the possible matches. Each match value follows a **case** keyword and employs a colon : character to associate one or more statements to be executed. Importantly, each **case** must end with a **break** statement to exit the **switch** statement after its associated statements have executed.

Optionally, a **switch** statement may include a final **default** alternative to associate one or more statements to be executed when none of the specified **case** values match the result of the expression evaluation.

So the syntax of a **switch** statement looks like this:

```
switch ( expression )
{
   case value-1 : statements-to-be-executed-when-matched ; break

   case value-2 : statements-to-be-executed-when-matched ; break

   case value-3 : statements-to-be-executed-when-matched ; break

   default : statements-to-be-executed-when-no-match-found
}
```

There is no limit to the number of **case** values that can be included within a **switch** statement block, so this is an ideal way to match any one of tens, hundreds, or even thousands of different values.

1 Create an HTML document with a self-invoking function that begins by declaring a variable
let day

switch.html

2 Next, insert a switch statement to assign a value to the variable following the evaluation of an expression
```
switch( 5 - 2 )
{
  case 1 : day = 'Monday' ; break

  case 2 : day = 'Tuesday' ; break

  case 3 : day = 'Wednesday' ; break

  case 4 : day = 'Thursday' ; break

  case 5 : day = 'Friday' ; break

  default : day = 'Weekend'
}
```

String values offered as possible **case** matches must be enclosed within quotes like all other string values.

3 Now, insert a statement to output the value assigned by the case statement that found a match
console.log('It is ' + day)

4 Save the HTML document, then open it in your browser and launch the console to see the assigned value in output

Loop For

A loop is a structure containing a test condition and one or more statements that are repeatedly executed while the test condition is met. Each single examination of the condition and execution of the statements is called an "iteration". When the test condition is not met, no further iterations are made and flow continues at the next statement following the loop structure.

Perhaps the most commonly used loop structure in JavaScript is the **for** loop, which has this syntax:

for (*initializer* ; *condition* ; *modifier*) { *statements-to-be-executed* }

The parentheses after the **for** keyword contain three expressions that control the number of iterations the loop will perform:

● **Initializer** – a statement that specifies the initial value of a variable that will be used to count the number of loop iterations . Traditionally, this trivial counter variable is simply named "i".

● **Condition** – an expression that is tested for a Boolean **true** value on each iteration. When the evaluation returns **true**, the loop statements are then executed to complete that iteration. If the evaluation returns **false**, the statements are not executed and the loop ends. Typically, the condition examines the value of the loop counter variable.

● **Modifier** – a statement that modifies a value in the test condition so that at some point its evaluation will return **false**. Typically, this will increment, or decrement, the loop counter variable.

For example, a **for** loop structure to execute a set of statements one hundred times might look like this:

let i
for (i = 0 ; i < 100 ; i++) { *statements-to-be-executed* }

In this case, the counter variable is incremented on each iteration until its value reaches 100, upon which the evaluation returns **false** and the loop ends.

Beware

Unless the modifier enables the evaluation to return **false** at some point, an infinite loop is created that will run forever.

...cont'd

1 Create an HTML document with a self-invoking function that begins by initializing a loop counter variable **let i = 0**

for.html

2 Next, insert a **for** loop structure that will make 10 iterations and output the value of the loop counter on each iteration

```
for( i = 1 ; i < 11 ; i++ )
{
  console.log( 'Iteration Number: ' + i )
}
```

3 Save the HTML document, then open it in your browser and launch the console to see the loop iterations

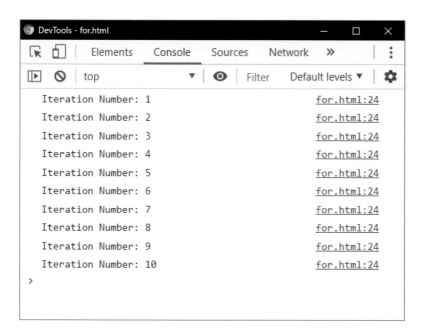

This is the regular **for** loop. There is also a special **for in** loop that is used to iterate through properties of an object and is demonstrated later, on page 66.

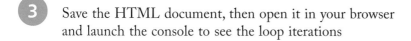

Loop While

The **for** loop structure, described on pages 52-53, is ideal when the number of required iterations is a known quantity, but when this is unknown a **while** loop structure is often preferable. The syntax of a **while** loop looks like this:

```
while( condition )
{
  statements-to-be-executed
  modifier
}
```

The parentheses after the **while** keyword contain a condition that is evaluated for a Boolean value upon each iteration. Statements to be executed on each iteration are enclosed within braces along with a statement that modifies a value in the test condition, so that at some point its evaluation will return **false** and the loop will exit. While the evaluation remains **true**, the statements will be executed on each iteration of the loop.

Where the condition evaluation is **false** on the first iteration, the loop exits immediately so the statements within its braces are never executed. Both **while** loops and **for** loops are sometimes referred to as "pre-test" loops because their test condition is evaluated before any statements are executed.

A **while** loop can be made to perform a specific number of iterations, like a **for** loop, by using a counter variable as the test condition and incrementing its value on each iteration. For example, a **while** loop structure to execute a set of statements 100 times might look like this:

```
let i = 0
while ( i < 100 )
{
  statements-to-be-executed
  i++ ;
}
```

The counter variable is incremented on each iteration until its value reaches 100, upon which the evaluation returns **false** and the loop ends.

Beware

Omitting a modifier from the **while** loop structure will create an infinite loop that will run forever.

1 Create an HTML document with a self-invoking function that begins by initializing a loop counter variable **let i = 10**

while.html

2 Next, insert a **while** loop structure that will make iterations and output the value of the loop counter on each iteration until it reaches zero
```
while( i > -1 )
{
  console.log( 'Countdown Number: ' + i )
  i--
}
```

3 Save the HTML document, then open it in your browser and launch the console to see the loop iterations

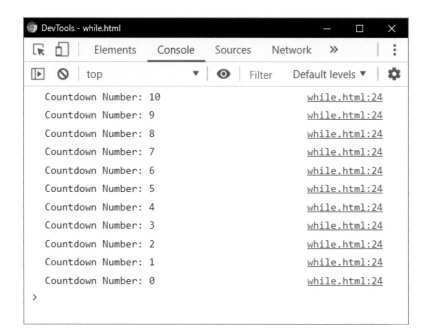

Hot tip

Each while loop must have braces as they contain at least two statements – one statement to execute and a modifier.

Do Loops

Another kind of loop available in JavaScript is the **do while** loop structure. This is like an inverted version of the **while** loop, described on pages 54-55, and is ideal when the statements it will execute on each iteration absolutely must be executed at least one time. Its syntax looks like this:

```
do
{
  statements-to-be-executed
  modifier
}
while ( condition )
```

The parentheses after the **while** keyword contain a condition that is evaluated for a Boolean value after each iteration. Statements to be executed on each iteration are enclosed within braces along with a statement that modifies a value in the test condition, so that at some point its evaluation will return **false** and the loop will exit. While the evaluation remains **true**, the statements will be executed on each iteration of the loop.

Where the condition evaluation is **false** on the first iteration, the loop exits immediately so the statements within its braces have been executed once. The **do while** loop is sometimes referred to as a "post-test" loop because the test condition is evaluated after its statements have been executed.

A **do while** loop can be made to perform a specific number of iterations, like a **for** loop, by using a counter variable as the test condition and incrementing its value on each iteration. For example, a **do while** loop structure to execute a set of statements 100 times might look like this:

```
let i = 0
do
{
  statements-to-be-executed
  i++
}
while ( i < 100 )
```

The counter variable is incremented on each iteration until its value reaches 100, upon which the evaluation returns **false** and the loop ends.

Hot tip

Only use a **do while** loop if the statements absolutely must be executed at least once.

...cont'd

1 Create an HTML document with a self-invoking function that begins by initializing a loop counter variable **let i = 2**

do.html

2 Next, insert a **do while** loop structure that will make iterations and output the value of the loop counter on each iteration until it exceeds 1000

```
do
{
  i *= 2
  console.log( 'Multiplied Number: ' + i )
}
while( i < 1000 )
```

3 Save the HTML document, then open it in your browser and launch the console to see the loop iterations

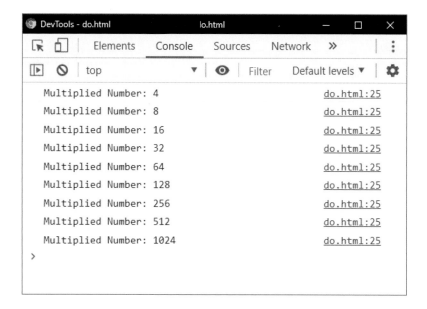

Notice that the final value exceeds the condition limit because it gets written in output before the test is made.

Break Out

The JavaScript **break** keyword can be used to exit from a loop when a specified condition is encountered. The conditional test should appear before all other statements to be executed so the loop will end immediately.

Where a **break** statement is used in a loop that is nested within an outer loop, flow resumes in the outer loop iteration.

The JavaScript **continue** keyword can be used to skip a single iteration of a loop when a specified condition is encountered.

Where a **continue** statement is used in a loop that is nested within an outer loop, flow resumes at the next iteration of the inner loop.

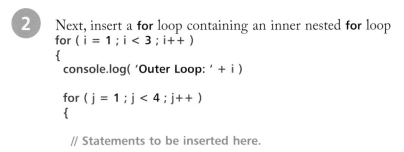

break.html

1 Create an HTML document with a self-invoking function that begins by initializing two loop counter variables
```
let i = 0
let j = 0
```

2 Next, insert a **for** loop containing an inner nested **for** loop
```
for ( i = 1 ; i < 3 ; i++ )
{
  console.log( 'Outer Loop: ' + i )

  for ( j = 1 ; j < 4 ; j++ )
  {

    // Statements to be inserted here.

    console.log( '\tInner Loop: ' + j )
  }

}
```

3 Save the HTML document, then open it in your browser and launch the console to see two iterations of the outer loop and three iterations of the inner loop

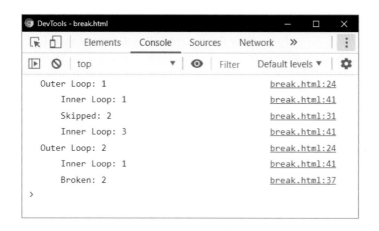

Don't forget

The **break** keyword is also used as a terminator in **switch** statements.

4 Next, insert statements in the inner loop to skip an iteration of the inner loop and break out of the outer loop

```
if( ( i === 1 ) && ( j === 2 ) ) {
  console.log( '\tSkipped: ' + j )
  continue
}

if( ( i === 2 ) && ( j === 2 ) ) {
  console.log( '\tBroken: ' + j )
  break
}
```

5 Save the HTML document again, then open it in your browser and launch the console to see an iteration skipped and the loop broken completely

Beware

Don't be tempted to use **break** statements to exit loops in place of the regular conditional tests that form part of the loop structure.

Catch Errors

Sections of script in which it is possible to anticipate errors, such as those handling user input, may be enclosed in a **try catch** structure to handle "exception" errors. The statements to be executed are contained within the braces of a **try** block, and exceptions are passed as an argument to the ensuing **catch** block for handling. Optionally, this may be followed by a **finally** block, containing statements to execute after exceptions have been handled.

JavaScript recognizes error objects of **Error, EvalError, InternalError, RangeError, ReferenceError, SyntaxError, TypeError**, and **URIError**. These may be automatically created and passed to the catch block by the parser or manually created with the **new** keyword and a constructor method, then passed using the **throw** keyword.

Each error object can have a **name** property and a **message** property to allow the **catch** block to describe its nature. The message is specified as an argument to the constructor for error objects created manually, but is predefined otherwise.

Alternatively, a string may be passed to the **catch** block by the **throw** keyword to identify the error. An appropriate action can then be determined by examining the string value.

catch.html

1. Create an HTML document with a self-invoking function that begins by initializing a variable
   let day = 32

2. Next, insert a **try** block to recognize invalid integer values
   ```
   try
   {
     if( day > 31 )
     {
       throw new RangeError( 'Day Cannot Exceed 31' )
     }

     if( day < 1 )
     {
       throw 'invalid'
     }
   }
   ```

③ Now, append a **catch** block to the **try** block, to handle invalid integer values

```
catch( err )
{
  if( err === 'invalid' )
  {
    console.log( 'Variable has invalid value of ' + day )
  }
  else
  {
    console.log( err.name + ' Exception: ' + err.message )
  }
}
```

④ Then, append a **finally** block to the **catch** block, to output a final message

```
finally
{
  console.log( 'The script has ignored the error...' )
}
```

⑤ Save the HTML document again, then open it in your browser and launch the console to see the error caught

Delete or comment-out the **day** variable declaration then save and refresh this example to see an automatic **ReferenceError** get caught.

⑥ Change the variable value to zero, then save the HTML document and refresh your browser to see the error caught

Summary

- The basic conditional test is performed with the **if** keyword to test a condition for a Boolean **true** or **false** value.

- An alternative branch to the basic conditional test can be provided by extending an **if** statement with the **else** keyword.

- A large number of conditions can be tested for a Boolean **true** or **false** value with a **switch** statement.

- In a **switch** block, each **case** statement must end with the **break** keyword to exit when a match is found.

- A **switch** block may contain a final **default** statement to execute when no match has been found.

- A **for** loop must specify an initializer, a condition to be tested for a Boolean **true** or **false** value, and a modifier.

- A loop modifier must enable the tested condition to become **false** at some point in order to exit the loop.

- The **while** loops and **for** loops evaluate a test condition before any statements are executed.

- A **do while** loop evaluates a test condition after its statements have been executed.

- The **break** keyword can be used to exit from a loop when a specified condition is encountered.

- The **continue** keyword can be used to skip a single iteration of a loop when a specified condition is encountered.

- The **try catch** structure can be used to handle exception errors that occur in a script.

- Each error object can have a **name** property and a **message** property to allow the **catch** block to describe its nature.

- A string may be passed to the **catch** block by the **throw** keyword to identify the error.

- A **try catch** structure may be followed by a **finally** block containing statements to execute after exceptions are handled.

4 Use Script Objects

The chapter describes how to create script objects and demonstrates how to use built-in JavaScript objects.

Custom Objects

Real-world objects are all around us, and they each have attributes and behaviors that we can describe:

- Attributes describe the features that an object has.

- Behaviors describe actions that an object can perform.

For example, a car might be described with attributes of "make" and "model", along with "accelerate" and "brake" behaviors.

These features could be represented in JavaScript with a custom **car** object containing variable properties of **make** and **model**, along with **accelerate( )** and **brake( )** methods.

Values are assigned to the object as a comma-separated list of name:value pairs within **{ }** curly brackets, like this:

```
let car = { make: 'Jeep', model: 'Wrangler',
  accelerate: function ( ) { return this.model + ' drives away' } ,
  brake: function ( ) { return this.make + ' pulls up' }
}
```

You can reference the object property values in two ways – using dot notation syntax of *objectName.propertyName* or using the syntax of *objectName['propertyName']*

The object methods can be called using dot notation syntax of *objectName.methodName( )*

The **this** keyword can be used in object method definitions to refer to the object that "owns" the method. In the example above, **this** refers to the **car** object, so **this.model** references the **car.model** property and **this.make** references the **car.make** property.

Hot tip

Whitespace is ignored in the object's list of name:value pairs, but don't forget to put a comma between the pairs.

1 Create an HTML document with a self-invoking function that begins by declaring a variable to contain an object definition
```
let car = {

  // Statements to be inserted here.

}
```

object.html

2 Next, insert statements to define the object's properties
```
make: 'Jeep' ,
model: 'Wrangler' ,
```

3 Now, insert statements to define the object's methods
```
accelerate: function ( ) {
  return this.model + ' drives away' } ,
brake: function ( ) {
  return this.make + ' pulls up' }
```

4 Then, after the closing **}** of the variable declaration, add a statement to output a string containing the object property values – using each reference technique
```
console.log( 'Car is a ' + car.make + ' ' + car[ 'model' ] )
```

5 Finally, add statements to call each object method
```
console.log( car.accelerate( ) )
console.log( car.brake( ) )
```

You must include the trailing **( )** parentheses to call a method, otherwise it will simply return the function definition.

6 Save the HTML document, then open it in your browser and launch the console to see the object's property values and the strings returned from its methods

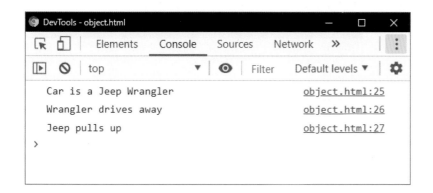

Extend Objects

Custom objects are very flexible and can easily be extended and updated at any time simply by assigning a new value, using dot notation to reference the property as **objectName.propertyName**

A special **for in** loop can be used to list all the property names and method names ('keys') of an object with this syntax:

for (*property* in *objectName*) { console.log(*property*) }

In order to reference the value of each property on each iteration, the property variable name can be enclosed within square brackets following the object name as **object-Name[*property*]**

extend.html

1 Create an HTML document with a self-invoking function that begins by initializing a variable that exactly recreates the object in the previous example

```
let property, car = {
  make: 'Jeep' ,
  model: 'Wrangler' ,
  accelerate: function ( ) {
    return this.model + ' drives away' } ,
  brake: function ( ) {
    return this.make + ' pulls up' }
}
```

2 Add a loop statement to list the name and value of each property and method

```
for( property in car ) {
  console.log( property + ': ' + car[ property ] )
}
```

Don't forget

The **property** variable in this example could, in fact, be given any valid variable name.

3 Save the HTML document, then open it in your browser and launch the console to see the object's keys and values

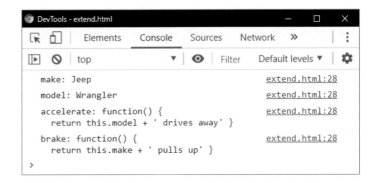

4 Next, add statements to assign new values to two existing object properties

```
car.make = 'Ford'
car.model = 'Bronco'
```

5 Now, add statements to extend the object with an additional property and an additional method

```
car.engine = 'V6'
car.start = function ( ) {
  return this.make + ' motor is running' }
```

6 Then, add statements to output strings containing the object property values – using each reference technique

```
console.log( '\nCar is a ' + car.make + ' ' + car[ 'model' ] )
console.log( 'Engine Type: ' + car.engine )
```

Hot tip

The **\n** escape sequence is used in this statement to include a newline (line break) in the output.

7 Finally, add statements to call each object method

```
console.log( car.start( ) )
console.log( car.accelerate( ) )
console.log( car.brake( ) )
```

8 Save the HTML document again, then refresh your browser to see the extended object's property values and the strings returned from its methods

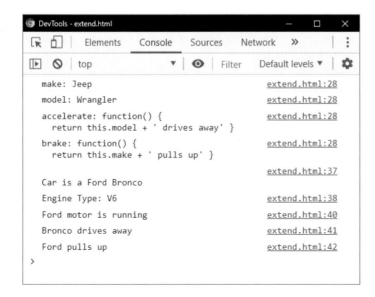

Built-in Objects

Object
String (an object only if created using the **new** keyword)
Number (an object only if created using the **new** keyword)
Boolean (an object only if created using the **new** keyword)
Object – an object defined by you
Date – an object containing date and time components
Array – an object storing indexed items of data
RegExp – an object describing a regular expression pattern
Math – an object providing math properties and methods
Error – an object supplying details of an error

Hot tip

If you're working through this book from the beginning you should already be somewhat familiar with **String**, **Number**, **Boolean**, **Error**, and **Object** objects. The **Array** object is introduced on page 70, the **Date** object is introduced on page 78, the **RegExp** object is introduced on page 86, and the **Math** object is introduced on page 90.

JavaScript provides the predefined built-in objects listed in the table above. Each of these objects, except for **Math**, has a like-named constructor method that can be used with the **new** keyword to create an object of that type – for example, to create a new **Date** object with **let now = new Date( )**.

It is, however, not recommended you use the **new** keyword and a constructor method for any object type other than **Error** and **Date**. JavaScript can intelligently recognize what type of object should be created by the value being assigned unless that value is a **string**, a **number**, or a **boolean**. These are each regarded as "primitive" literal values that have no properties or methods, so a **typeof** statement returns **string, number, boolean,** for these – not **object**.

All JavaScript built-in objects inherit properties and methods from a top-level **Object.prototype** object. For example, this provides a **toLocaleString( )** method to lower-level objects such as **Date.prototype**, so you can append that method call to a **Date** object to get a locally formatted date string.

You can also call inherited methods on the primitive **string, number,** and **boolean** literal values because JavaScript will automatically call the method from the equivalent object. This means you can append the **toLocaleString( )** method call to a **number** literal value to get a locally formatted number string.

...cont'd

1 Create an HTML document with a self-invoking function that begins by assigning primitive literal values to three variables

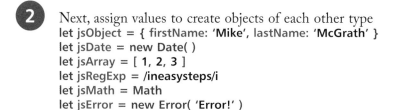

```
let jsString = 'Text'      // not, new String( 'Text' ).

let jsNumber = 125000 // not, new Number( 125000 ).

let jsBoolean = true       // not, new Boolean( true ).
```

builtin.html

2 Next, assign values to create objects of each other type

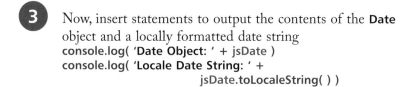

```
let jsObject = { firstName: 'Mike', lastName: 'McGrath' }
let jsDate = new Date( )
let jsArray = [ 1, 2, 3 ]
let jsRegExp = /ineasysteps/i
let jsMath = Math
let jsError = new Error( 'Error!' )
```

The **Math** object is the only JavaScript object that does not provide a constructor method.

3 Now, insert statements to output the contents of the **Date** object and a locally formatted date string

```
console.log( 'Date Object: ' + jsDate )
console.log( 'Locale Date String: ' +
                          jsDate.toLocaleString( ) )
```

4 Then, insert statements to output the primitive literal **number** value and a locally formatted numeric string

```
console.log( '\nPrimitive Number: ' + jsNumber )
console.log( 'Locale Number String: ' +
                          jsNumber.toLocaleString( ) )
```

5 Save the HTML document, then open it in your browser and launch the console to see the output strings

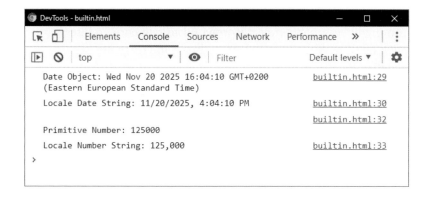

69

Create Arrays

An **Array** object is a JavaScript built-in object that can store multiple items (of various data-types) in individual "elements". An array is created by assigning [ ] square brackets to a variable, which can optionally contain a comma-separated list of values to initialize the array elements. Its syntax looks like this:

let *arrayName* = [*value1* , *value2* , *value3*]

Unlike custom objects, where each property is named, array elements are automatically numbered – starting at zero. So the first element is 0, the second is 1, the third is 2, and so on. This numbering system is often referred to as a "zero-based index".

The value stored within an array element can be referenced by enclosing its element index number within square brackets following the object name. For example, **colors[0]** would reference the value in the first element in an array named "colors".

Where array elements are not required to be initialized immediately, an empty array can be created and values assigned to its elements later, like this:

let colors = [ ]

colors[0] = 'Red'

colors[1] = 'Green'

colors[2] = 'Blue'

Although the Array object provides an **Array( )** constructor it should not be used as it can produce unexpected results – for example, creating an array initializing the first element, like this:

let jsArray = new Array(10)

You might reasonably expect **jsArray[0]** to reference an integer value of 10 within the first element, but it in fact returns an **undefined** value. What's going on? This is an anomaly that only occurs when you specify a single integer argument to the constructor method – which causes JavaScript to create an array of 10 empty elements! Creating the array with **jsArray = [10]** does not have that effect, and creates the array with its first element containing the integer value of 10 as expected.

Don't forget

All built-in object names begin with an uppercase character – so the constructor is named "Array", not "array".

70

1 Create an HTML document with a self-invoking function that begins by creating an array – the wrong way
```
let jsArray = new Array( 10 )
```

array.html

2 Next, add statements to output the value in the first array element and list the entire array
```
console.log( jsArray[ 0 ] )
console.log( jsArray )
```

3 Now, add a statement to declare a variable, and to declare a variable initialized with an array
```
let month, summer = [ 'June', 'July', 'August' ]
```

4 Then, add a loop to output the index number and value of each array element
```
for ( month in summer )
{
  if ( month !== ' ' )
  {
    console.log( month + ': ' + summer[ month ] )
  }
}
```

Hot tip

It's good practice to wrap the body of **for in** loops in an **if** statement – here, it ensures the element is not empty.

71

5 Finally add statements to output the value in the first array element and list the entire array
```
console.log( 'Start of Summer: ' + summer[ 0 ] )
console.log( summer )
```

6 Save the HTML document, then open it in your browser and launch the console to see the array element contents

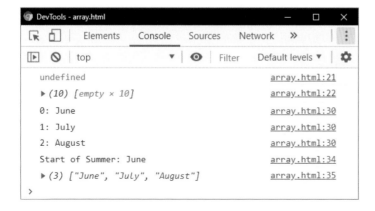

```
DevTools - array.html                              —  □  ×
  ⬚  ⬚ │ Elements  Console  Sources  Network  »  │  ⋮
  ▶  ⊘ │ top              ▼ │ ⊙ │ Filter  Default levels ▼ │ ⚙
    undefined                              array.html:21
  ▶ (10) [empty × 10]                      array.html:22
    0: June                                array.html:30
    1: July                                array.html:30
    2: August                              array.html:30
    Start of Summer: June                  array.html:34
  ▶ (3) ["June", "July", "August"]         array.html:35
  >
```

Loop Elements

Arrays and loops make great partners! Any kind of loop can be used to fill the elements of an array with values. The elements of even very large arrays can be "populated" in this way – and with surprisingly little code.

Similarly, loops can be used to quickly read the values in each array element and perform some action appropriate to that value on each iteration of the loop.

Usefully, each array has a **length** property that contains an integer record of the total number of elements in that array. As a result of zero-based indexing this will always be one greater than the final element's index number, so can be readily used in a conditional test to terminate the loop.

elements.html

1 Create an HTML document with a self-invoking function that begins by declaring three variables
let i, result, boolArray = [ ]

2 Next, output a simple heading
console.log('Fill Elements...')

3 Now, add a loop to fill 10 elements with Boolean values and output their index number and each stored value
```
for( i = 1 ; i < 11 ; i++ )
{
  boolArray[ i ] = ( i % 2 === 0 ) ? true : false
  console.log( 'Element ' + i + ': ' + boolArray[ i ] )
}
```

4 Then, output a second simple heading and initialize a variable with an empty string value
```
console.log( 'Read Elements...' )
result = ''
```

5 Next, add a loop to assign the index numbers of any elements containing a **true** value to a string
```
for( i = 1 ; i < boolArray.length ; i++ )
{
  if( boolArray[ i ] ) { result += i + ' | ' }
}
```

Hot tip

This array **length** property here has a value of 11 because the array has eleven elements – even though element zero has not been filled.

6 Now, output the string to reveal the index numbers of elements that contain a **true** value
```
console.log( 'True in Elements: ' + result )
```

7 Reset the string variable to contain an empty string
```
result = ''
```

8 Then, add a loop to assign the index numbers of any elements containing a **false** value to a string
```
for( i = 1 ; i < boolArray.length ; i++ )
{
  if( !boolArray[ i ] ) { result += i + ' | ' }
}
```

9 Finally, output the string to reveal the index numbers of elements that contain a **false** value
```
console.log( 'False in Elements: ' + result )
```

10 Save the HTML document, then open it in your browser and launch the console to write and read array elements

Conditional tests for a Boolean value do not need to include the expression **=== true** as that is automatic.

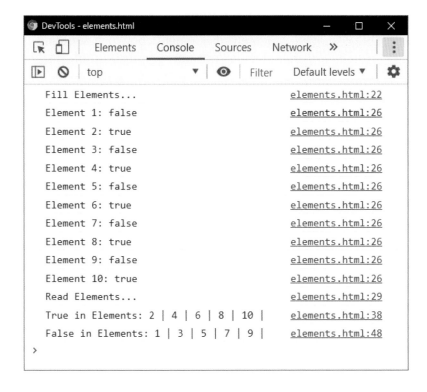

```
DevTools - elements.html                          —    □    ✕

 ⌞⋆  ⭧  │  Elements   Console   Sources   Network  »   │  ⋮

 ▷  ⊘  │ top              ▼ │ ◉ │ Filter   Default levels ▼ │ ⚙

  Fill Elements...                          elements.html:22
  Element 1: false                          elements.html:26
  Element 2: true                           elements.html:26
  Element 3: false                          elements.html:26
  Element 4: true                           elements.html:26
  Element 5: false                          elements.html:26
  Element 6: true                           elements.html:26
  Element 7: false                          elements.html:26
  Element 8: true                           elements.html:26
  Element 9: false                          elements.html:26
  Element 10: true                          elements.html:26
  Read Elements...                          elements.html:29
  True in Elements: 2 | 4 | 6 | 8 | 10 |    elements.html:38
  False in Elements: 1 | 3 | 5 | 7 | 9 |    elements.html:48
 ›
```

Slice Arrays

JavaScript objects have properties and methods. In addition to the **length** property, each array object has methods that can be used to manipulate the elements in an array. These are listed in the table below, together with a brief description of the task they perform:

Method	Description
join(*separator*)	Unites all element values into a single string separated by a specified separator, or by a comma if no separator is specified
pop( )	Deletes the last element of the array, and returns its value
push(*value* , *value*)	Adds elements to the end of the array and returns the new length
reverse( )	Reverses the order of all elements in the array and returns the reordered value of each element
shift( )	Deletes the first element of the array, and returns its value
slice(*begin* , *end*)	Returns elements between specified index positions, or the end of the array if no end position is specified
sort( )	Sorts all elements in the array into alphabetical or numerical order and returns the reordered value of each element
splice(*position* , *number*, *value*, *value*)	Replaces a specified number of element values starting at a specified index position, and returns the replaced values
unshift(*value* , *value*)	Adds elements to the start of the array and returns the new length

Hot tip

The **join( )** method is faster for uniting a large number of element values into a single string, but the + concatenate operator is faster at uniting just a few element values.

Beware

The **slice( )** method returns the element values up to, but not including, the optional end index position.

74

Where no values are specified by the **push( )** or **unshift( )** methods, a single empty element gets added to the array. A comma-separated list of values can be specified to the **push( )**, **unshift( )**, and **splice( )** methods to change multiple elements.

1 Create an HTML document with a self-invoking function that begins by creating an array
```
let seasons = [ 'Spring', 'Summer', 'Fall', 'Winter' ]
console.log( 'Elements: ' + seasons )
```

slice.html

2 Next, output a modified list of the elements
```
console.log( 'Joined: ' + seasons.join( ' & ' ) )
```

3 Now, extract the final element from the array
```
console.log( 'Popped: ' + seasons.pop( ) )
console.log( 'Elements: ' + seasons )
```

Hot tip

4 Then, put the final element back on the array
```
console.log( 'Pushed: ' + seasons.push( 'Winter' ) )
console.log( 'Elements: ' + seasons )
```

Use the **slice( )** method without a replacement value to delete a specified number of elements at a specified position and it will automatically renumber all remaining elements that follow in that array.

5 Next, output just two element values
```
console.log( 'Sliced: ' + seasons.slice( 1, 3 ) )
```

6 Finally, replace the value in the third element
```
console.log( 'Spliced: ' + seasons.splice( 2, 1, 'Autumn' ) )
console.log( 'Elements: ' + seasons )
```

7 Save the HTML document, then open it in your browser and launch the console to see the elements manipulated

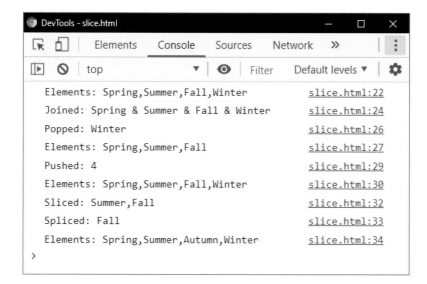

Don't forget

The **shift( )** and the **unshift( )** methods work like **pop( )** and **push( )** but on the first element rather than the last. The **reverse( )** and **sort( )** methods are used in the next example listed on pages 76-77.

Sort Elements

It is often desirable to arrange an array's element values in a particular order using the array **sort( )** method. This can optionally specify a comparison function argument to define the sort order.

When no comparison function is specified, the **sort( )** method will, by default, convert all element values to strings then sort them lexicographically in dictionary order – comparing each first character, then each second character, and so on. Where the elements contain matching strings that differ only by character case, the string with most uppercase characters gets a lower index position – appearing before that with fewer uppercase characters.

The **sort( )** method's default behavior of sorting into dictionary order is usually satisfactory for string values but is often not what you want when sorting numerical values. For example, in sorting three values 30, 100, 20, the result is 100, 20, 30 – because the first characters are different they are sorted by that comparison only. Typically, it is preferable to require all numerical element values to be sorted in ascending, or descending, numerical order so the **sort( )** method needs to specify the name of a custom comparison function to define the sort order.

A comparison function nominated by the **sort( )** method will be passed successive pairs of element values for comparison, and it must return an integer value to indicate each comparison's result. When the first value is greater than the second it should return a value greater than zero to indicate that the first value should be sorted to a higher index position – to appear after the second value. Conversely, the comparison function should return a value less than zero to indicate that the first value should be sorted to a lower index position – to appear before the second value. When both values are identical, zero should be returned to indicate that the element positions should remain unchanged. When all comparisons have been made, the elements will be arranged in ascending value order. If descending order is required, the array's **reverse( )** method can then be used to reverse the element order.

If a comparison function is comparing numerical element values it simply needs to return the result of subtracting the second passed value from the first passed value to have the desired effect.

Remember that **sort( )** does actually rearrange the values stored in the array elements.

The default behavior of the **sort( )** method is the equivalent of a comparison function comparing arguments **x** and **y** with these statements:
**if(x > y) return 1
else if(x < y) return -1
else return 0**.

1 Create an HTML document with a self-invoking function that begins by creating two arrays
```
let hues = [ 'Red', 'RED', 'red', 'Green', 'Blue' ]
let nums = [ 1, 20, 3, 17, 14, 0.5 ]
```

sort.html

2 Next, output the values in each array, and output their element values sorted in dictionary sort order
```
console.log( 'Colors: ' + hues )
console.log( 'Dictionary Sort: ' + hues.sort( ) )
console.log( '\nNumbers: ' + nums )
console.log( 'Dictionary Sort: ' + nums.sort( ) )
```

3 Now, add a statement to output the numerical values sorted after calling a comparison function
```
console.log( 'Numerical Sort: ' + nums.sort( sortNums ) )
```

4 Finally, in the function block, add a statement to output the numerical values in descending order
```
console.log( 'Reversed Sort: ' + nums.reverse( ) )
```

5 Next, in the script, add the comparison function
```
function sortNums( numOne, numTwo ) {
  return numOne - numTwo
}
```

6 Save the HTML document, then open it in your browser and launch the console to see the elements sorted

Beware

When the **sort( )** method specifies a comparison function it must nominate it by function name only – do not include trailing brackets after the comparison function name in the argument to the **sort( )** method.

Get Dates

The built-in JavaScript **Date** object provides components representing a particular date, time, and timezone. An instance of a **Date** object is created using the **new** keyword, a **Date( )** object constructor, and a variable name assignment. Without specifying any arguments to the constructor, a new **Date** object represents the date and time of its creation based upon the system time of the computer on which the browser is running. There is no consideration given as to whether system time is accurate to the Universal Time Clock (UTC) or Greenwich Mean Time (GMT).

Computer date and time is measured numerically as the period of elapsed time since January 1, 1970 00:00:00 – a point in time often referred to as the "epoch". In JavaScript, the elapsed time is recorded as the number of milliseconds since the epoch. This figure can be extracted from **Date** object using its **getTime( )** method, and may be subtracted from that of another **Date** object to calculate an elapsed period between two points in a script – for example, to calculate the period taken to execute a loop.

A string of the components within a **Date** object can be extracted using its **toString( )** method, or an equivalent converted to UTC time using its **toUTCString( )** method.

JavaScript can determine in which time zone the user is located, assuming the system is correctly set to the local time zone, by examining the value returned by a current **Date** object's **getTimezoneOffset( )** method. This returns an integer value that is the number of minutes by which the current local time differs from UTC time. The calculation is performed in minutes rather than hours because some time zones are offset by other than one-hour intervals – for example, Newfoundland, Canada is UTC -3:30 (UTC -2:30 during periods of daylight saving time).

The time zone offset value can be used to provide localized customization for U.S. time zones but they must be adjusted by subtracting 60 (minutes) for periods of daylight saving time. The example opposite calls **getMonth( )** and **getDate( )** methods of a **Date** object to adjust the time zone offset value if daylight saving time is not in operation at the current date.

Hot tip

More examples follow on pages 80-85 that demonstrate how to use components of a **Date** object by calling its many methods.

1 Create an HTML document with a self-invoking function that begins by initializing three variables
```
const now = new Date( )
let offset = now.getTimezoneOffset( )
let dst = 60
```

date.html

2 Next, add statements to turn off daylight saving time from November 3 to March 10
```
if( ( now.getMonth( ) < 3 ) && ( now.getDate( ) < 10 ) )
{ dst = 0 }
if( ( now.getMonth( ) > 9 ) && ( now.getDate( ) > 2 ) )
{ dst = 0 }
```

Beware

The **getMonth( )** method returns a zero-based index number in which March is at position 2 – more on this in the next example on pages 80-81.

3 Now, add a statement to establish a time zone
```
switch( offset )
{
  case ( 300 - dst ) : offset = 'East Coast' ; break
  case ( 360 - dst ) : offset = 'Central' ; break
  case ( 420 - dst ) : offset = 'Mountain' ; break
  case ( 480 - dst ) : offset = 'Pacific' ; break
  default : offset = 'All'
}
```

4 Finally, add statements to output date and time information, and an appropriate greeting message
```
console.log( 'System Time: ' + now.toString( ) )
console.log( 'UTC (GMT) Time: ' + now.toUTCString( ) )
console.log( '\nWelcome to ' + offset + ' Visitors' )
```

Hot tip

Discovery of the user's local time zone could be used to direct the browser to a page relevant to that time zone – for example, a page containing only Californian distributors for users in the Pacific time zone. But be aware that system time information can be easily changed by the user to any time, date, or time zone, so may not necessarily report their actual location.

5 Save the HTML document, then open it in your browser and launch the console to see the elements sorted

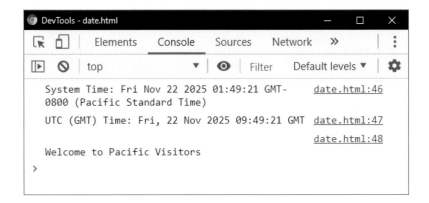

Extract Calendar

A JavaScript **Date** object provides separate methods to extract each of its date components for the year, month name, day of the month, and the day name:

Method	Returns
getFullYear( )	Year as four digits (yyyy)
getMonth( )	Month as index number (0-11)
getDate( )	Day as number (1-31)
getDay( )	Weekday as index number (0-6)

The **Date** object's **getFullYear( )** method returns the year as a four-digit number, such as **2025**, and the **Date** object's **getDate( )** method returns the day number of the month – so that on the first day of the month it returns **1**.

For reasons of internationalization, **getMonth( )** and **getDay( )** return index number values that must be converted to the local language month and day names by the script. The conversion is easily made for month names by creating an array of all month names, starting with January, then using the index number returned by **getMonth( )** to reference the appropriate month name from the array element.

Similarly, the conversion is made for day names by creating an array of all day names, starting with Sunday, then using the index number returned by the **getDay( )** method to reference the appropriate day name from the array element.

The various components can then be assembled into a date string arranged according to the preferred date format of any locale.

1 Create an HTML document with a self-invoking function that begins by initializing three variables

```
const days = [ 'Sun', 'Mon', 'Tue', 'Wed', 'Thu', 'Fri', 'Sat' ]
const months = [ 'Jan', 'Feb', 'Mar', 'Apr', 'May', 'Jun',
                 'Jul', 'Aug', 'Sep', 'Oct', 'Nov', 'Dec' ]
const now = new Date( )
```

calendar.html

2 Next, add statements to extract individual date components using methods of the **Date** object

```
let year = now.getFullYear( )
let month = now.getMonth( )
let dayNumber = now.getDate( )
let dayName = now.getDay( )
```

3 Now, add statements to convert the extracted index numbers to month name and day name values

```
month = months[ month ]
dayName = days[ dayName ]
```

4 Then, concatenate the date components into date strings – in both American and British date formats

```
let usDate = dayName + ', ' + month + ' ' +
             dayNumber + ', ' + year

let ukDate = dayName + ', ' + dayNumber + ' ' +
             month + ', ' + year
```

5 Finally, add statements to output each date string

```
console.log( 'U.S. Date: ' + usDate )
console.log( 'U.K. Date: ' + ukDate )
```

6 Save the HTML document, then open it in your browser and launch the console to see the formatted date strings

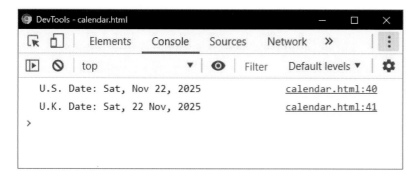

Month indexing starts at zero (0), not one (1) – so for example March is at index [2] not at [3].

Extract Time

A JavaScript **Date** object provides separate methods to extract each of its time components for the hour, the minute, the second, and the millisecond:

Method	Returns
getHours( )	Hour as number (0-23)
getMinutes( )	Minute as number (0-59)
getSeconds( )	Second as number (0-59)
getMilliseconds( )	Millisecond as number (0-999)

Beware

Time components are based upon the user's system time – which may not be accurate.

The **Date** object's **getHours( )** method returns the hour in 24-hour format – as a value in the range 0-23. The **getMinutes( )** and **getSeconds( )** methods both return a value in the range 0-59. There is also a **getMilliseconds( )** method for even greater precision that returns a value in the range 0-999.

The values of each component can be concatenated into a time string but it is often preferable to add a leading zero to single minute and second values for better readability. For example, 10:05:02 is preferable to 10:5:2.

An appropriate greeting string can be created by examining the hour value to establish whether the user's system time is currently morning, afternoon, or evening.

For situations where a 12-hour time format is desirable, an "AM" or "PM" suffix can be created by examining the hour value and all PM hour values reduced by 12. For example, 13:00 can be transformed to 1:00 PM.

HTML

time.html

 Create an HTML document with a self-invoking function that begins by initializing five variables

```
const now = new Date( )
let hour = now.getHours( )
let minute = now.getMinutes( )
let second = now.getSeconds( )
let millisecond = now.getMilliseconds( )
```

...cont'd

2 Next, add statements to prefix a zero to minute and second values below 10

```
if( minute < 10 ) { minute = '0' + minute }
if( second < 10 ) { second = '0' + second }
```

3 Now, concatenate the time components into a string, then output that string

```
let time = 'It is now: ' + hour + ':' + minute + ':' +
        second + ' and ' + millisecond + ' milliseconds'
console.log( time )
```

Hot tip

The **Date** object also provides methods to retrieve the UTC equivalent of each date and time component – for example, methods **getUTCMonth( )**, and **getUTCHours( )**.

4 Then, output a greeting appropriate to the current time add statements to output each date string

```
let greeting = 'Good Morning!'
if( hour > 11 ) { greeting = 'Good Afternoon!' }
if( hour > 17 ) { greeting = 'Good Evening!' }
console.log( greeting )
```

5 Finally, output the time in a 12-hour format

```
let suffix = ( hour > 11 ) ? ' P.M.' : ' A.M.'
if( hour > 12 ) { hour -= 12 }
console.log( 'Time is: ' + hour +':' + minute + suffix )
```

6 Save the HTML document, then open it in your browser and launch the console to see the formatted time strings

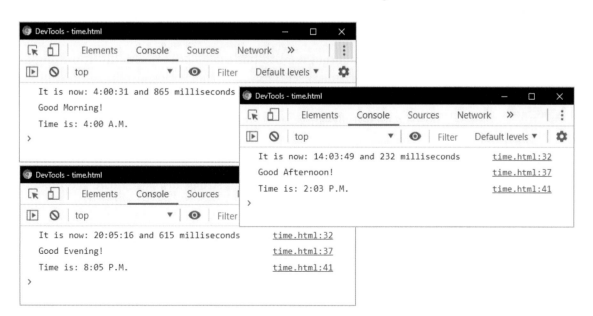

Set Dates

The JavaScript **Date( )** constructor can optionally specify two to seven arguments to set values for each of its components, like this:

new Date(*year, month, date, hours, minutes, seconds, milliseconds* **)**

When only the minimum year and month are specified, the date component is set to one (1), and all time components are set to zero (0).

The **Date** object also provides separate methods to specify the value of each of its date and time components individually:

Method	Sets
setDate( )	Day as number (1-31)
setFullYear( )	Year as four digits (yyyy)
setMonth( )	Month as number (0-11)
setHours( )	Hour as number (0-23)
setMinutes( )	Minute as number (0-59)
setSeconds( )	Second as number (0-59)
setMilliseconds( )	Millisecond as number (0-999)

The **setMonth( )** method sets the month numerically in the range where 0=January-11=December and, optionally, the **setFullYear( )** method can also set the month and day using this syntax:

*date.***setFullYear(** *year , monthNumber , dayNumber* **)**

The values of each set component can be revealed by displaying the entire **Date** object. Additionally, all **Date** objects have methods to output a variety of strings displaying date and time. The **toString( )** method converts the date to a string value; the **toUTCString( )** method converts the date to its UTC equivalent; and the **toLocaleString( )** method displays the date using the computer's locale conventions. Useful **toDateString( )** and **toTimeString( )** methods can display date and time components.

Hot tip

The **toString( )** method returns the string value of any JavaScript object and has many uses.

84

1 Create an HTML document with a self-invoking function that begins by creating a 4th-of-July **Date** object

```
const holiday = new Date( 2025, 6, 4 )
console.log( 'Object: ' + holiday )
```

setdate.html

2 Next, add statements to modify individual date components to become a Christmas Day at noon

```
holiday.setFullYear( 2028 )
holiday.setMonth( 11 )
holiday.setDate( 25 )
holiday.setHours( 12 )
holiday.setMinutes( 0 )
holiday.setSeconds( 0 )
holiday.setMilliseconds( 0 )
```

3 Now, add statements to output the modified date and time and its equivalent UTC (GMT) time

```
console.log( 'String: ' + holiday.toString( ) )
console.log( 'UTC: ' + holiday.toUTCString( ) )
```

Hot tip

The **Date** object also has a **setTime( )** method that accepts an argument of the number of milliseconds since the epoch – each day has 86,400,000 milliseconds, so **setTime(86400000)** sets the date Jan 1, 1970.

85

4 Then, add statements to output the modified date and time in locale string, date string, and time string formats

```
console.log( 'Locale: ' + holiday.toLocaleString( ) )
console.log( 'Date: ' + holiday.toDateString( ) )
console.log( 'Time: ' + holiday.toTimeString( ) )
```

5 Save the HTML document, then open it in your browser and launch the console to see set date and time strings

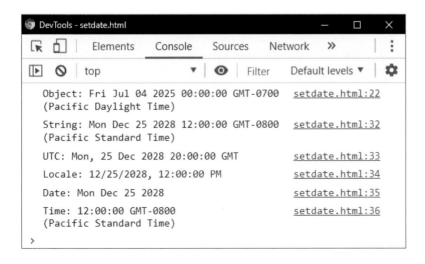

Match Patterns

The **RegExp** object is a JavaScript built-in object that can contain a "regular expression" pattern – describing a string of characters. Regular expressions are useful for text validation and for search-and-replace operations within text by matching their specified pattern to a section of the text.

A regular expression pattern may consist entirely of literal characters between **/ /** describing a character string to match. For example, the regular expression **/wind/** finds a match in "<u>wind</u>ows" – the pattern quite literally matches the string in the text. More typically, a regular expression pattern consists of a combination of literal characters and these "metacharacters":

Beware

The topic of regular expressions is extensive and beyond the remit of this book – but a brief introduction is provided here for completeness.

Metacharacter	Matches	Example
.	Any Characters	ja..pt
^	First Characters	^ja
$	Final Characters	....pt$
*	Zero Or More Repetitions	ja*
+	One Or More Repetitions	ja+
?	Zero Or One Repetition	ja?
{ }	Multiple Repetitions	ja{ 3 }
[ ]	Character Class	[a-z]
\	Any Digits	\d
|	Either Optional Character	a | b
( )	Expression Group	(...)

Don't forget

The character class **[a-z]** matches only lowercase characters but **[a-z0-9]** also matches digits.

The pattern may also include an **i** modifier after the final **/** character, to perform a case-insensitive search, or a **g** modifier to perform a global search for all matches of the pattern.

A **RegExp** object has a **test( )** method that returns **true** when a match is found, or **false** otherwise. A **RegExp** object also has an **exec( )** method that returns a **null** value if no match was found, or the text found if the search was successful, and its **index** property, which contains the character position where the match begins.

...cont'd

1 Create an HTML document with a self-invoking function that begins by initializing three variables
`const system = 'Windows', suite = 'Office' pattern = /ice/i`

regexp.html

2 Next, add statements to output two search results
```
console.log( 'In ' + system +'? ' + pattern.test( system ) )
console.log( 'In ' + suite + '? ' + pattern.test( suite ) )
```

3 Now, add statements to output the text match and position, or a message if unsuccessful
```
let result = pattern.exec( suite )
if( result )
{
  console.log( 'Found ' + result + ' at ' + result.index )
}
else { console.log( 'No Match Found' ) }
```

4 Then, add statements to output the result of an attempt to validate a badly formatted email address
```
let email = 'mike@example'
const format = /.+\@.+\..+/
console.log( email + ' Valid? ' + format.test( email ) )
```

The regular expression used here tests only the most basic email format requirements.

5 Finally, add statements to correct the address format and output the validation result
```
email += '.com'
console.log( email + ' Valid? ' + format.test( email ) )
```

6 Save the HTML document, then open it in your browser and launch the console to see regular expression matches

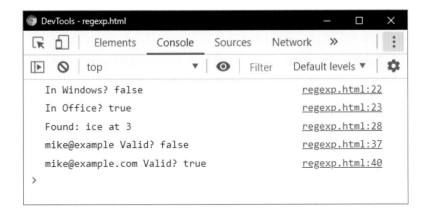

```
DevTools - regexp.html                                    —  □  ✕

  ▯         Elements   Console   Sources   Network   »        ⋮

 ▢  ⊘  | top              ▼ | ⊙ | Filter  Default levels ▼  | ✿

   In Windows? false                          regexp.html:22
   In Office? true                            regexp.html:23
   Found: ice at 3                            regexp.html:28
   mike@example Valid? false                  regexp.html:37
   mike@example.com Valid? true               regexp.html:40
 >
```

The character index begins at zero, so the fourth character is at index position 3.

Summary

- Values are assigned to a custom object as a comma-separated list of name:value pairs within **{ }** curly brackets.

- Object property values can be referenced using dot notation syntax or by quoting their name between **[ ]** square brackets.

- Object methods are called by appending **( )** parentheses after the object's method name.

- The **this** keyword can be used in object method definitions to refer to the object that owns the method.

- Custom objects can be extended by assigning a new value using dot notation to reference the property.

- A **for in** loop can be used to list all property names and method names of an object.

- All JavaScript built-in objects inherit properties and methods from a top-level **Object.prototype** object.

- The JavaScript built-in **Array** object store items in individual elements that are numbered starting at zero.

- Values can be assigned to an array as a comma-separated list within **[ ]** square brackets.

- The value in an array element is referenced by enclosing its index number in **[ ]** square brackets after the object name.

- Each **Array** object has a length property and methods that can be used to manipulate the elements in the array.

- The JavaScript built-in **Date** object provides separate methods to extract each of its date and time components.

- The JavaScript **Date( )** constructor can optionally specify two to seven arguments to set values for each of its components.

- The **Date** object also provides separate methods to set the value of each of its date and time components individually.

- The JavaScript built-in **RegExp** object can contain a regular expression pattern that describes a string of characters.

- The **RegExp** object has **test( )** and **exec( )** methods that search a specified string argument for a match to its pattern.

5 Control Numbers & Strings

Calculate Areas

JavaScript has a built-in **Math** object that provides a number of useful methods and constant mathematical values. The constants are listed in the table below, together with their approximate value:

Constant	Description
Math.E	Constant E, base of the natural logarithm, with an approximate value of 2.71828
Math.LN2	The natural logarithm of 2, with an approximate value of 0.69315
Math.LN10	The natural logarithm of 10, with an approximate value of 2.30259
Math.LOG2E	The base-2 logarithm of constant E, with an approximate value of 1.44269
Math.LOG10E	The base-10 logarithm of constant E, with an approximate value of 0.43429
Math.PI	The constant PI, with an approximate value of 3.14159
Math.SQRT1_2	The square root of 0.5, with an approximate value of 0.70711
Math.SQRT2	The square root of 2, with an approximate value of 1.41421

Hot tip

All the **Math** methods are listed on page 92.

There is no need to create an instance of the **Math** object as it is globally available by default, so **Math** constants and methods are accessible from anywhere in your script via the **Math** object and dot notation syntax.

The **Math** constants are mostly used in scripts that have a particular mathematical purpose, but all the **Math** constants are listed above for completeness.

...cont'd

1 Create an HTML document with a self-invoking function that begins by initializing a variable
```
let radius = 4
console.log( '\nRadius of Circle: ' + radius )
```

constants.html

2 Next, add statements to perform a mathematical calculation and display the result in output
```
let area = Math.PI * ( radius * radius )
console.log( '\nArea of Circle: ' + area )
```

3 Now, add statements to perform another mathematical calculation and display the result in output
```
let circumference = 2 * ( Math.PI * radius )
console.log( '\nPerimeter of Circle: ' + circumference )
```

4 Then, add statements to perform a final mathematical calculation and display the result in output
```
let cube = ( radius * radius * radius )
let volume = ( ( 4 / 3 ) * Math.PI ) * cube
console.log( '\nVolume of Sphere: ' + volume )
```

5 Save the HTML document, then open it in your browser and launch the console to see the mathematical results

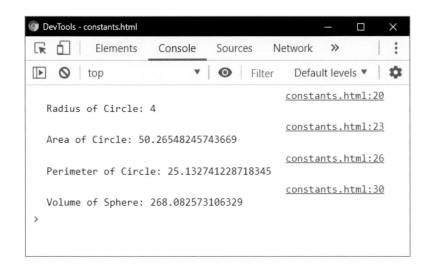

All **Math** constant names must be stated in uppercase – for example, be sure to use **Math.PI** rather than **Math.pi**.

Compare Numbers

The built-in **Math** object provides these useful methods:

Method	Returns
Math.abs( )	An absolute value
Math.acos( )	An arc cosine value
Math.asin( )	An arc sine value
Math.atan( )	An arc tangent value
Math.atan2( )	An angle from an X-axis point
Math.ceil( )	A rounded-up value
Math.cos( )	A cosine value
Math.exp( )	An exponent of constant E
Math.floor( )	A rounded-down value
Math.log( )	A natural logarithm value
Math.max( )	The larger of two numbers
Math.min( )	The smaller of two numbers
Math.pow( )	A power value
Math.random( )	A pseudo-random number
Math.round( )	The nearest integer value
Math.sin( )	A sine value
Math.sqrt( )	A square root value
Math.tan( )	A tangent value

...cont'd

1 Create an HTML document with a self-invoking function that begins by initializing two variables

```
let square = Math.pow( 5, 2 )    // 5 to power 2 ( 5 x 5 )

let cube = Math.pow( 4, 3 )      // 4 to power 3 ( 4 x 4 x 4 )
```

math.html

2 Next, add statements to display the largest and smallest of these two positive variable values in output

```
console.log( '\nLargest Positive: ' +
                         Math.max( square, cube ) )
console.log( '\nSmallest Positive: ' +
                         Math.min( square, cube ) )
```

3 Now, add statements to reverse the numerical polarity of each variable – making positive values into negative values

```
square *= -1
cube *= -1
```

4 Then, add statements to display the largest and smallest of these two negative variable values in output

```
console.log( '\nLargest Negative: ' +
                         Math.max( square, cube ) )
console.log( '\nSmallest Negative: ' +
                         Math.min( square, cube ) )
```

5 Save the HTML document, then open it in your browser and launch the console to see the numerical comparisons

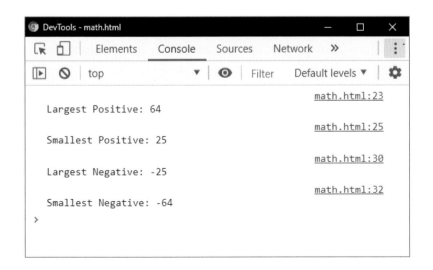

The largest negative value is the one closest to zero.

Round Decimals

The built-in JavaScript **Math** object provides three methods for rounding floating-point numbers to integer values. Each method takes the floating-point value as its argument and returns an integer. The **Math.ceil( )** method rounds up, the **Math.floor( )** method rounds down, and the **Math.round( )** method rounds up or down to the nearest integer.

When handling floating-point values it is important to recognize a discrepancy that exists between the prevailing computer floating-point math standard, as defined by the IEEE (Institute of Electrical and Electronics Engineers), and generally accepted mathematical accuracy. This exists because some decimal numbers cannot be exactly translated into binary form. For example, the decimal number 81.66 cannot be exactly translated to binary – so the expression **81.66 * 15** returns **1224.8999999999999** rather than the mathematically accurate figure of **1224.9**.

Some programming languages provide automatic rounding to overcome floating-point discrepancies, but JavaScript does not so care must be taken, especially with monetary values, to avoid mathematically erroneous results. The recommended procedure is to first multiply the floating-point value by 100, then perform the arithmetical operation, and finally divide the result by 100 to return to the same decimal level.

A similar procedure can be used to commute long floating-point values to just two decimal places. After multiplying a value by 100, the **Math.round( )** method can be employed to round the value, then division by zero returns to two decimal places.

Procedures that multiply, operate, then divide, can be written as individual steps or parentheses can be used to determine the order in a single succinct expression. For example, commuting a long floating-point value in a variable named "num" can be written as:

```
num = num * 100
num= Math.round( num )
num /= 100
```

or alternatively as:

```
num = ( Math.round( num * 100 ) ) / 100
```

Hot tip

The **Math.round( )** method rounds up by default – so **Math.round(7.5)** returns 8, not 7 and **Math.round(-7.5)** returns -7, not -8.

1 Create an HTML document with a self-invoking function that begins by initializing a variable
`let bodyTemp = 98.6`

round.html

2 Next, add statements to display closest integers to the floating-point value
```
console.log( 'Ceiling: ' + Math.ceil( bodyTemp ) )
console.log( 'Floor: ' + Math.floor( bodyTemp ) )
console.log( 'Round: ' + Math.round( bodyTemp ) )
```

3 Now, add statements to display an incorrectly calculated result of an expression and a corrected equivalent
```
console.log( '\nImprecision: ' + ( 81.66 * 15 ) )

console.log( 'Corrected: ' + ( ( ( 81.66 * 100 ) * 15 ) / 100 ) )
```

4 Then, add statements to display a long floating-point value and a commuted equivalent
```
console.log( '\nFloat: ' + Math.PI )

console.log( 'Commuted: ' +
                ( ( Math.round ( Math.PI * 100 ) / 100 ) ) )
```

5 Save the HTML document, then open it in your browser and launch the console to see the rounded numbers

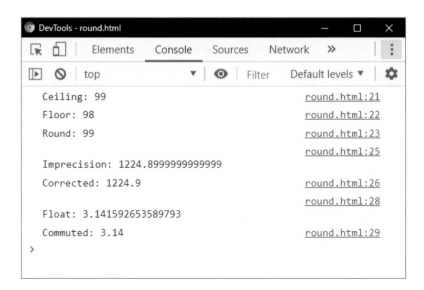

Expressions in innermost parentheses are evaluated first.

Generate Randoms

The JavaScript **Math.random( )** method returns a random floating-point number between 0.0 and 1.0. This can be used for a variety of web page effects that require a generated random number. Multiplying the random floating-point value will increase its range. For example, multiplying it by 10 increases the range to become 0.0-10.0.

Generally, it is useful to round the random value up with the **Math.ceil( )** method so that the range becomes 1-10.

The process of specifying the range for a random number value can be written as individual steps, or parentheses can be used to determine the order in a single expression. For example, specifying a range of 1-10 for a variable named "rand" can be written as:

```
let rand = Math.random( )
rand *= 10
rand = Math.ceil( rand )
```

or alternatively as:

```
let rand = Math.ceil( Math.random( ) * 10 )
```

A series of unique random numbers can be generated within a specified range. For example, to produce a random lottery numbers selection within the range 1-59:

random.html

① Create an HTML document with a self-invoking function that begins by declaring five variables
```
let i, rand, temp, nums = [ ]
let str = '\n\nYour Six Lucky Numbers: '
```

② Next, add a loop to fill array elements 1-59 with their respective index number
```
for( i = 1 ; i < 60 ; i++ ) { nums[ i ] = i }
```

Hot tip

Step 3 contains an algorithm that shuffles the numbers and ensures no two elements contain the same number.

③ Now, add a loop to randomize the numbers in the array elements
```
for( i = 1 ; i < 60 ; i++ )
{
  rand = Math.ceil( Math.random( ) * 59 )
  temp = nums[ i ]
  nums[ i ] = nums[ rand ]
  nums[ rand ] = temp
}
```

4 Then, add a loop to append a hyphenated list of six
element values to the string variable
```
for( i = 1 ; i < 7 ; i++ )
{
  str += nums[ i ]
  if( i !== 6 ) { str += ' - ' }
}
```

5 Finally, add a statement to output the string variable
```
console.log( str )
```

6 Save the HTML document, then open it in your browser
and launch the console to see a unique selection of
random numbers within the specified range each time the
script is executed

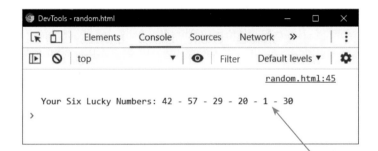

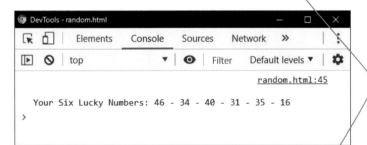

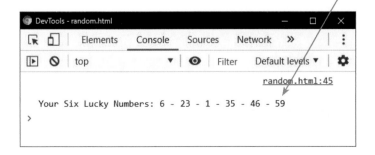

Here, the random
numbers are in the range
1 to 59 – to play the UK
Lotto game or the US
New York Lotto game.

Unite Strings

JavaScript has a **String** object that provides useful methods to manipulate string values. There is, however, no need to create instances of the **String** object with the **new** keyword and the **String( )** constructor, as its methods can simply be applied to string variables using dot notation. For example, **str.toUpperCase( )** returns all characters of a string variable named "str" in uppercase, whereas **str.toLowerCase( )** returns all its characters in lowercase.

There is also a string **length** property that stores the total number of characters in a string.

Many of the examples listed earlier use the **+** concatenation operator to unite multiple strings but, alternatively, the string **concat( )** method can be used to append one or more strings supplied as a comma-separated list of arguments.

The **eval( )** built-in function is also used to unite strings and variables by some script authors – but this absolutely should be avoided. The **eval( )** function directly calls the JavaScript compiler to compile its string argument into a JavaScript statement:

- If the string represents an expression, **eval( )** will evaluate that expression – for example, **eval('1 + 1')** returns 2.

- If the string represents a statement, or sequence of statements, **eval( )** will evaluate the last statement – for example, the code **eval('let num = 100 ; alert(num)')** produces an alert dialog.

```
This page says
100
                                          OK
```

This use of **eval( )** incurs a large cost in script performance and is unnecessary in almost every case as there is usually a more efficient and elegant solution. Furthermore, the **eval( )** function can have security implications if the script allows user input to be evaluated as a JavaScript instruction. This provides the opportunity to execute malicious code. For example, the code **eval('while(true) ; alert( )')** will produce an infinite loop that locks the browser.

① Create an HTML document with a self-invoking function that begins by declaring three variables
```
let topic = 'JavaScript'
let series = 'in easy steps'
let title = ''
```

string.html

② Next, add statements to display converted case versions of the first two string variable values
```
console.log( topic + ' > ' + topic.toLowerCase( ) )
console.log( series + ' > ' + series.toUpperCase( ) )
```

③ Now, add statements to append a space and the second string onto the first string, then assign it to the third variable and output the concatenated string
```
title = topic.concat( ' ', series )
console.log( 'Title: ' + title )
```

④ Then, add statements to display the length of each string in output
```
console.log( '\n' + topic + ' - Length: ' + topic.length )

console.log( series + ' - Length: ' + series.length )

console.log( title + ' - Length: ' + title.length )
```

⑤ Save the HTML document, then open it in your browser and launch the console to see the string output

Split Strings

There are several string methods that allow a specified part of a string to be copied from the full string. These treat each string like an array, in which each element contains a character or a space, and can be referenced by their index position. As with arrays, the string index is zero-based, so the first character is at position zero.

The start at which to begin copying a "substring" can be specified by stating its index position as an argument to the string's **substring( )** method. This will copy all characters after that position right up to the end of the string. Optionally, a second argument may be supplied to the string's **substring( )** method to specify a subsequent index position as the end of the substring. This will then copy all characters between the start and end positions.

An alternative way to copy substrings is provided by the string **substr( )** method. Like the **substring( )** method, this can take a single argument to specify the index position at which to begin copying, and will copy all characters after that position right up to the end of the string. Unlike the **substring( )** method, the **substr( )** method may optionally be supplied with a second argument to specify the number of characters to copy after the start position.

Similarly, the string **slice( )** method can be used to return all characters after a start position, specified by a single argument, or all characters between two positions, specified as two arguments.

It is sometimes useful to copy parts of a string that are separated by a particular character. The separator character can be specified as an argument to the string **split( )** method, which will return an array of all substrings that exist between occurrences of that character. Optionally, the **split( )** method may be supplied with a second argument specifying the size of the array it should return. In this case, each substring that exists between the specified separator character is returned until the limit is reached, and the rest of the string is ignored.

None of these string methods modify the original string but merely make a copy of a particular part of the original string.

The **substr( )** method is invariably easier to use than the **substring( )** method – because you need only calculate the start position and the substring length, not an end position.

The **split( )** method is used to separate cookie data in the example on page 138.

1 Create an HTML document with a self-invoking function that begins by initializing a variable
```
let definition = 'JavaScript is the original dialect of \
the ECMAScript standard language.'
```

split.html

2 Next, add statements to assign selected slices of the string to a second variable, then output its value
```
let str = definition.slice( 0, 27 )
str += definition.slice( 62, 70 )
console.log( str )
```

Hot tip

A \ backslash character lets you continue the string on the next line.

3 Now, add a statements to output four individual words of the slices
```
console.log( str.split( ' ', 4 )
```

4 Then, add statements to assign selected substrings of the original string to the second variable, then output its value
```
str = definition.substring( 42, 52 )
str += definition.substring( 10, 17 )
str += definition.substr( 52, 70 )

console.log( str )
```

5 Save the HTML document, then open it in your browser and launch the console to see the split string output

Don't forget

Specify '' (an empty string without any space) as the separator to the **split( )** function to return an array of individual characters.

Find Characters

The JavaScript **String** object provides a number of methods that allow a string to be searched for a particular character or substring. The string **search( )** method takes a substring as its argument and returns the position at which that occurs in the searched string, or a **-1** value if it is not found. Alternatively, the substring can be specified as the argument to a string **match( )** method that will return the substring if it is present, or the JavaScript **null** value if it is absent.

The string **indexOf( )** method takes a substring as its argument and returns the index position of the first occurrence of the substring when it's present, or **-1** when it's absent. The **lastIndexOf( )** method works in the same way but searches backwards, from the end of the string, reporting the last occurrence of the substring.

To discover the character at a particular index position in a string, its index value can be specified as an argument to a **charAt( )** method, or its numerical Unicode value can be revealed by specifying its index value to the **charCodeAt( )** method. Conversely, one or more Unicode values can be specified as arguments to the **String.fromCharCode( )** method to return their character values.

Additionally, all occurrences of a character or substring can be replaced by specifying their value as the first argument to the string **replace( )** method, and a replacement value as its second argument.

Beware

The **null** keyword is not equivalent to a zero value, as **null** has no value whatsoever.

find.html

Hot tip

Use double quotes to include quote marks in a string surrounded by single quotes.

1. Create an HTML document with a self-invoking function that begins by initializing a variable with a string value
   let str = 'JavaScript in easy steps'

2. Next, add statements to output the results of two case-sensitive string searches
   console.log('"Script" Search: ' + str.search('Script'))
   console.log('"script" Search: ' + str.search('script'))

3. Now, add statements to output the results of two case-sensitive string matches
   console.log('\n"Script" Match: ' + str.match('Script'))
   console.log('"script" Match: ' + str.match('script'))

4 Add statements to output the first and last index positions of a character if found within the string
```
console.log( '\nindexOf "s": ' + str.indexOf( 's' ) )
console.log( 'indexOf "m": ' + str.indexOf( 'm' ) )
console.log( '\nlastIndexOf "s": ' + str.lastIndexOf( 's' ) )
console.log( 'lastIndexOf "m": ' + str.lastIndexOf( 'm' ) )
```

Hot tip

Unicode uppercase A-Z values are 65-90, and lowercase a-z values are 97-122.

5 Then, add statements to output the first character in the string and its Unicode value, plus four characters specified by their Unicode values
```
console.log( '\ncharAt 0: ' + str.charAt( 0 ) )
console.log( 'charCodeAt 0: ' + str.charCodeAt( 0 ) )
console.log( 'fromCharCode: ' +
          String.fromCharCode( 74, 97, 118, 97 ) )
```

6 Finally, add statements to output the original string and a modified version of that string
```
console.log( '\nOriginal: ' + str )
console.log( 'Replaced: ' + str.replace( 'easy', 'simple' ) )
```

7 Save the HTML document, then open it in your browser and launch the console to see the results output

Don't forget

The **replace( )** method returns a modified version of the original string but does not actually change the original string.

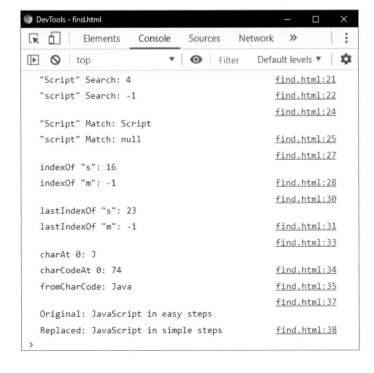

Trim Strings

The JavaScript **String** object provides a **trim( )** method that removes whitespace from both ends of a string. This is especially useful to ensure that user input does not have spaces, tabs, or newline characters accidentally included by the user.

Having trimmed whitespace from a string, you can verify its first characters using a **startsWith( )** method, and verify its last characters using an **endsWith( )** method. These each accept a character or substring as their argument and seek a case-sensitive match within the string. If a match is found they will return **true**, otherwise they will return **false** if no match is found.

An individual character can be referenced by stating its index position within [ ] square brackets after the string variable name – for example, **str[0]** to reference the first letter of a string in a variable named "str".

You can also perform a case-sensitive match within a string by specifying a character or substring as the argument to an **includes( )** method. If a match is found, this will return **true**, otherwise it will return **false** if no match is found.

If you wish to construct a new string containing multiple copies of an existing string, simply specify an integer argument to a **repeat( )** method to determine how many times the existing string should be repeated in the newly created string.

Hot tip

The **split( )** method is used to remove whitespace from cookie data in the example on page 139.

trim.html

1. Create an HTML document with a self-invoking function that begins by initializing a variable – with a value that contains whitespace at both ends of a string
    `let str = '   Love For All, Hatred For None.   '`

2. Next, add statements to output the string and test its beginning and end
    ```
    console.log( 'String: ' + str )
    console.log( 'Starts With "L" ? ' + str.startsWith( 'L' ) )
    console.log( 'Ends With "." ? ' +str.endsWith( '.' ) )
    console.log( 'First Letter: ' + str[ 0 ] )
    ```

3. Now, add a statement to assign a trimmed version of the string to the variable
    `str = str.trim( )`

4 Then, add statements to output the trimmed string and
   test its beginning and end, as before
   ```
   console.log( 'Trimmed: ' + str )
   console.log( 'Starts With "L" ? ' + str.startsWith( 'L' ) )
   console.log( 'Ends With "." ? ' +str.endsWith( '.' ) )
   console.log( 'First Letter: ' + str[ 0 ] )
   ```

5 Add statements to see substrings within the string
   ```
   console.log( '\nIncludes "Hat" ? '+ str.includes( 'Hat' ) )
   console.log( 'Includes "hat" ? '+ str.includes( 'hat' ) )
   ```

6 Finally, add a statement to output 10 copies of the
   trimmed string
   ```
   console.log( '\nRepeat:\n' + str.repeat( 10 ) )
   ```

7 Save the HTML document, then open it in your browser
   and launch the console to see the results output

Character matching
can alternatively be
performed with the
equality operator, such
as **str[0] === 'L'**

Matching with these
methods is case-
sensitive.

Summary

- The **Math** object provides mathematical constants, such as **Math.PI**, and mathematical methods, such as **Math.max( )**

- Floating-point numbers can be rounded to the nearest integer using **Math.floor( )**, **Math.ceil( )**, and **Math.round( )** methods.

- JavaScript does not provide automatic rounding to overcome floating-point discrepancies.

- Multiply floating-point values by 100, perform the arithmetic, then divide the result by 100 to avoid discrepancy errors.

- The **Math.random( )** method returns a random floating-point number between 0.0 and 1.0.

- Multiplying a random floating-point number by 10 and rounding the result with **Math.ceil( )** makes the range 1-10.

- The **String** object provides useful methods to manipulate string values, such as **toUpperCase( )** and **toLowerCase( )**

- Each string has a **length** property containing an integer that is the total number of characters in that string.

- Strings can be joined together using the + concatenation operator or the string **concat( )** method.

- The **eval( )** built-in function can have security implications so is best avoided.

- The **slice( )** and **substring( )** method arguments specify start and end positions, but those of the **substr( )** method specify the start position and the number of characters to copy.

- The **split( )** method returns an array of all substrings that exist between occurrences of the character specified as its argument.

- The **search( )**, **match( )**, **indexOf( )**, **lastIndexOf( )**, and **charAt( )** methods can be used to seek characters within a string.

- The **trim( )** method removes whitespace from both ends of a string.

- The **startsWith( )**, **endsWith( )**, and **includes( )** methods seek a case-sensitive match within a string.

- The **replace( )** and **repeat( )** methods create modified strings.

6 Address the Window Object

Meet DOM

The browser represents all components of a web page within a hierarchical tree called the "Document Object Model" (DOM). Each component appears below the top-level **window** object, and the tree contains branches like those illustrated below:

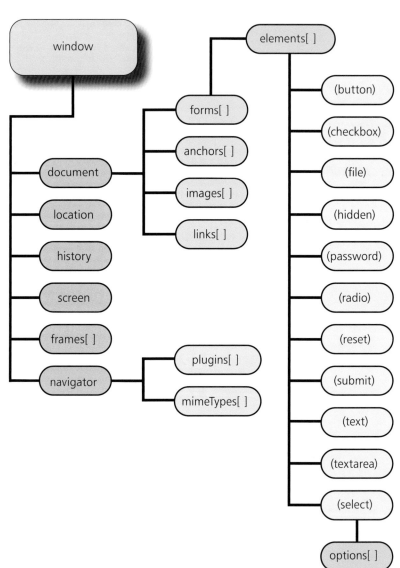

Hot tip

Items followed by square brackets are array objects, and those within regular parentheses are various types of form elements.

A **for in** loop can be used to list all properties of the **window** object provided by the browser. The list will contain fundamental properties that are common to all modern browsers, plus minor properties that are browser-specific.

1 Create an HTML document with an empty list element
`<ol id="props" style="column-count:3"> </ol>`

dom.html

2 Next, in a script element, create a self-invoking function that begins by initializing two variables
```
const list = document.getElementById( 'props' )
let property = null
```

3 Now, add a loop to populate the list element with items that are direct properties of the browser's **window** object
```
for( property in window )
{
  if( property ) { list.innerHTML += '<li>' + property }
}
```

Closing **</li>** tags are optional so are omitted in this loop.

4 Save the HTML document, then open it in your browser to see the **window** object's properties and method names

Scroll down the list to examine all **window** properties and methods – on this occasion there was a total of 204 items. The important properties in the tree illustration opposite are highlighted in this screenshot.

Inspect Properties

The top-level DOM **window** object has a **screen** child object that provides properties describing the user's monitor resolution in pixel measurement. Overall screen dimensions can be found in the **window.screen.width** and **window.screen.height** properties.

Similarly, the usable screen dimensions, excluding the space occupied by the desktop task bar, can be found in the **window.screen.availWidth** and **window.screen.availHeight** properties.

The screen's color capability can be discovered from the **window.screen.colorDepth** property that contains a bit value describing the range of possible colors that screen can display:

Notice the "camelCase" capitalization of these property names.

- **8-bit** – Low Color can display only 256 colors.

- **16-bit** – High Color can display 65,536 colors.

- **24-bit** – True Color can display millions of colors.

- **32-bit** – Deep Color can display a gamut comprising a billion or more colors.

Modern computers use 24-bit or 32-bit hardware for color display, but older computers use 16-bit hardware. Only very old computers and old cellphones use 8-bit hardware for color display.

There is also a **window.screen.pixelDepth** property that contains the screen's pixel depth, but on modern computers this is the same value as in the **window.screen.colorDepth** property – always use **window.screen.colorDepth** to discover the color capability.

Some browsers now support a **window.screen.orientation** object that has a **type** property describing the current orientation of the screen as either landscape or portrait, and whether this is the screen's primary or secondary usual orientation.

As the **window** object is the top-level global object in the browser's scripting environment, its name can optionally be omitted when referencing its child objects and their properties. For example, you can simply write **screen.colorDepth** to reference the **window.screen.colorDepth** property.

1 Create an HTML document with an empty paragraph
```
<p id="props" style="font:1.5em sans-serif"></p>
```

screen.html

2 Next, in a script element, create a self-invoking function that begins by initializing six variables
```
const info = document.getElementById( 'props' )
let width = window.screen.width + 'px'
let height = window.screen.height + 'px'
let availW = window.screen.availWidth + 'px'
let availH = window.screen.availHeight + 'px'
let colors = 'Unknown'
```

3 Now, add a statement to describe the color capability
```
switch( window.screen.colorDepth )
{
  case 8 : colors = 'Low Color' ; break
  case 16 : colors = 'High Color' ; break
  case 24 : colors = 'True Color' ; break
  case 32 : colors = 'Deep Color' ; break
}
```

The **colorDepth** property can be used to deliver low resolution images within a document for browsers with limited color capabilities.

4 Then, add statements to display screen information
```
info.innerHTML  = 'Screen Resolution: ' +
                  width + ' x ' + height + '<br>'
info.innerHTML += 'Available Screen Size: ' +
                  availW + ' x ' + availH + '<br>'
info.innerHTML += 'Color Capability: ' + colors + '<br>'
if( window.screen.orientation )
{
  info.innerHTML += 'Orientation: ' +
                  window.screen.orientation.type
}
```

5 Save the HTML document, then open it in your browser to see the screen information

The available height here is 40 pixels less than the screen height because the desktop taskbar is 40 pixels high.

Show Dialogs

The top-level DOM **window** object provides three methods with which JavaScript can display dialog messages to the user. A simple warning message string can be specified as the argument to the **window.alert( )** method. This gets displayed on a dialog box with just an "OK" button, which merely closes the dialog box.

More usefully, a message can be specified as the argument to the **window.confirm( )** method to request a decision from the user. This gets displayed on a dialog box with an "OK" button and a "Cancel" button. Either button will close the dialog box when pushed, but the "OK" button returns a **true** value, whereas the "Cancel" button returns a **false** value.

A message can also be specified as the argument to the **window.prompt( )** method to request input from the user. This gets displayed on a dialog box with an "OK" button, a "Cancel" button, and a text input field. Either button will close the dialog box when pushed, but the "OK" button returns the value in the text field, whereas the "Cancel" button returns a **null** value. A second argument can also be supplied to the **window.prompt( )** method to specify default content for the text field.

dialogs.html

1 Create an HTML document with an empty paragraph
<p id="response" style="font:1.5em sans-serif"></p>

2 Next, in a script element, create a self-invoking function that begins by initializing one variable reference
const info = document.getElementById('response')

3 Now, add a statement to display a message on a simple dialog box
window.alert('Hello from JavaScript')

4 Then, add a statement to request a decision from the user and write the response in the paragraph
**info.innerHTML = 'Confirm: ' +
        window.confirm('Go or Stop?')**

5 Next, add a statement to request text input from the user and write the text response into the paragraph
**info.innerHTML += '
Prompt: ' +
        window.prompt('Yes or No?', 'Yes')**

6 Save the HTML document, then open it in your browser to see the message appear on a simple dialog box

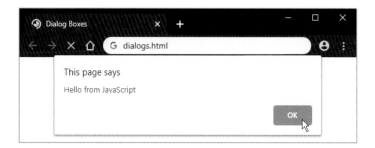

7 Click the OK button on each dialog box to close them in turn, then see the response appear in the paragraph

Hot tip

The **confirm** dialog can be used with an **if** statement to branch a script – for example, **if(confirm('OK?')) { ... } else { ... }**

Don't forget

If the script is to use text input from a **prompt** dialog it is good practice to trim whitespace from the ends of the string – see page 104.

Scroll Around

The DOM **window** object has a **scrollBy( )** method that allows the window to be scrolled horizontally and vertically when content overflows the window in either orientation. This method requires two arguments to specify the number of pixels to shift along the X and Y axes.

When content overflows the window vertically, a scroll bar appears along the right edge of the browser window. The **scrollBy( )** method will scroll by the number of pixels specified as its first argument – or until it reaches the extreme of the content.

Similarly, when content overflows the window horizontally, a scroll bar appears along the bottom of the browser window. The **scrollBy( )** method will scroll by the number of pixels specified as its second argument – or until it reaches the extreme of the content.

There is also a **scrollTo( )** method that accepts two arguments specifying X and Y coordinates that the top-left corner of the window should scroll to when content overflows the window horizontally and vertically. This can be used to shift away from the default X=0, Y=0 coordinates to a specified alternative position. For example, where the browser is displaying data in a tabular spreadsheet format, with the first cell of the first row in the top left corner of the browser window, the **scrollTo( )** method can place a particular cell at the top-left corner of the browser window instead.

The DOM **window** object has a **scrollX** property that stores the number of pixels by which the window is scrolled horizontally. This denotes the position of the "thumb" (scroller box) along the scrollbar at the bottom of the window, relative to its left corner. The **window.scrollX** property is an alias for an older property named **window.pageXOffset** that still exists in the DOM, and can be used instead of **window.scrollX** for backward compatibility.

Similarly, there is a **scrollY** property that stores the number of pixels by which the window is scrolled vertically. This denotes the position of the thumb along the scrollbar at the right of the window, relative to its top corner. The **window.scrollY** property is an alias for an older property named **window.pageYOffset** that still exists in the DOM, and can be used instead of **window.scrollY** for backward compatibility.

Hot tip

Supply negative values to the **scrollBy( )** method to move up and left.

Beware

The effect of the **scrollby( )** method is only apparent when the content overflows the window – causing scroll bars to appear.

...cont'd

1 Create an HTML document with a wide empty paragraph that is inset from the left of the window
```
<p id="info" style="width:2000px; margin-left:300px;
                    font:1.2em sans-serif"></p>
```

scroll.html

2 Next, in a script element, create a self-invoking function that begins by initializing two variables
```
const info = document.getElementById( 'info' )
let i = 0
```

3 Now, add a loop to write a column of 40 numbers into the paragraph
```
for( i = 1 ; i < 41 ; i++ )
{
  info.innerHTML += ( i + '<br>' )
}
```

4 Then, add a statement to scroll the widow 200 pixels horizontally to the right, and by the height of the paragraph element vertically downward
```
window.scrollBy( 200, info.clientHeight )
```

Hot tip

Notice the use of the element's **clientHeight** property here. Elements also have a useful **clientWidth** property.

5 Finally, add a statement to append a confirmation of the current window's thumb positions
```
info.innerHTML += 'scrollX: ' + window.scrollX +
                  '& scrollY: ' + window.scrollY
```

6 Save the HTML document, then open it in your browser to see the window scroll and thumb positions

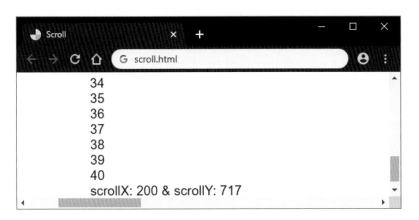

Pop-up Windows

A new browser window can be opened using the **window** object's **open( )** method. This requires three arguments to specify the URL address of the HTML document to be loaded in the new window, a name for the new window, and a comma-separated list of features that the window should include – from the possible features described in the table below:

Feature	Description
directories	Adds the links bar
height	Sets height in pixels of the document area
left	The screen X coordinate of the window
location	Adds the address bar
menubar	Adds the standard menu bar
resizable	Permits the window to be resized
scrollbars	Enables scrollbars when needed
status	Adds the status bar
toolbar	Adds the Forward and Back buttons bar
top	The screen Y coordinate of the window
width	Sets width in pixels of the document area

Browser makers have added Pop-up Blockers due to the annoying proliferation of pop-up windows – so the use of pop-ups is no longer recommended, but they are demonstrated here for completeness.

When successful, the **window.open( )** method returns a new **window** object and opens the new "pop-up" window or if it fails, the method simply returns **null**. The returned result should be assigned to a variable that may be subsequently tested – if the variable is not **null** it must then represent the pop-up window object. That window may then be closed by calling its **close( )** method, or its contents printed by calling its **print( )** method.

Windows can also be positioned by specifying X and Y screen axes coordinates as arguments to a **window.moveTo( )** method. There is also a similar **window.moveBy( )** method that accepts two arguments to specify how many pixels along the X and Y axes the window should be shifted from its current screen position.

1 Create an HTML document containing a heading
`<h1>`**Pop-up Window**`</h1>`

popup.html   opener.html

2 Create a second HTML document containing a heading
`<h1>`**Main Window**`</h1>`

3 Next, within a script element in the second document,
add a self-invoking function that creates a window object
**const popWin = window.open('popup.html', 'Popup',
'top=150,left=100,width=350,height=100')**

Beware

Do not put any spaces
in the features list string
as it may cause the
window.open( ) method
to fail.

4 Save both HTML
documents, then open the
second document to see its
pop-up window is blocked

5 Open the browser's
Pop-up Blocker dialog
and choose to allow
pop-ups from this page

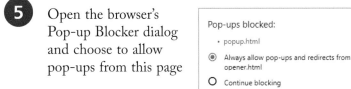

6 Now, refresh the
browser window to see
the pop-up window appear with the specified features

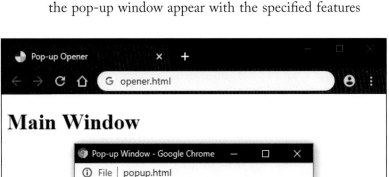

Hot tip

Notice that the pop-up
window does not display
the specified "favicon"
on its title bar.

Make Timers

The JavaScript **window** object has an interesting **setTimeout( )** method that can repeatedly evaluate a specified expression after a specified period of time. Where the specified expression calls the function in which the **window.setTimout( )** statement appears, a recursive loop is created – in which the function is repeatedly executed after the specified period of time.

The expression to be evaluated by the **setTimeout( )** method must be specified as its first argument, and the period of time must be a number specified as its second argument. The time is expressed in milliseconds, where 1000 represents one second.

The **setTimeout( )** method returns a numeric value that can be assigned to a variable to uniquely identify the waiting process. This value can be specified as the argument to the window object's **clearTimeout( )** method to terminate the timer loop at some point.

A two-minute task set to an interval of 10 minutes gets started every 10 minutes, but the same task set to a timeout of 10 minutes gets started every 12 minutes (10+2).

The **window** object also has **setInterval( )** and **clearInterval( )** methods that take the same arguments and work in a similar way. The difference is that the time specified to **setInterval( )** specifies the interval at which point the expression is to be evaluated, irrespective of how long it takes to execute. Conversely, the time specified to the **setTimeout( )** method specifies the period of time between the end of one execution until the start of the next execution. This means that it is possible for **setInterval( )** to attempt overlapping executions where the interval is short and the time taken to execute the expression is lengthy. For this reason it is generally preferable to use the **setTimeout( )** method.

1 Create an HTML document with an empty paragraph
<p id="info"></p>

2 Next, in a script element, initialize a variable with a closure function that returns a decreasing integer
const count = (function ( ) {

```
let num = 10
return ( function( ) { return num-- } )

} ) ( )
```

timer.html

For a refresher on closure functions see page 24.

3 Now, add a timer function that begins by initializing three variables

```
function countDown( )
{
  const info = document.getElementById( 'info' )
  let timerId = null
  let num = count( )
  // Statements to be inserted here.
}
```

4 Insert statements to write the decreasing integer into the paragraph at one-second intervals until it reaches zero

```
if ( num > 0 )
{
  info.innerHTML += '<span>'+ num + '</span>'
  timerId = window.setTimeout( countDown , 1000 )
}
else
{
  info.innerHTML += '<span>Lift Off!</span>'
  window.clearTimeout( timerId )
}
```

Hot tip

You could usefully add a **console.log(timerId)** statement to the timer function to see the timer's ID value.

5 After the function block, add a statement to call the timer function when the page has loaded

```
countDown( )
```

6 Save the HTML document, then open it in your browser to see the timer count down for 10 seconds

Examine Browsers

In the DOM hierarchy, the top-level **window** object has a number of child objects, which each have their own properties and methods. One of these is the **window.navigator** object that contains information about the web browser. As the top-level **window** object exists in the "global namespace", all its child objects can omit that part of the address, so the **window.alert( )** method can be simply called using **alert( )**, the **window.onload** property can be referenced using **onload**, and the **window. navigator** object can be referenced using **navigator**.

The **navigator** object has an **appName** property that contains the browser name, an **appCodeName** property that contains its code name, and an **appVersion** property that contains its version number. But you may be surprised with the values as Google Chrome, Firefox, Safari, and Opera all give their code name as "Mozilla".

Each browser sends the browser code name and version in a HTTP header named "User-Agent" when making a request to a web server, and this string can also be retrieved from the **navigator.userAgent** property. There is also a **navigator.platform** property that describes the browser's host operating system.

In previous years, much was made of browser detection scripts that attempted to identify the browser using its **navigator** properties so that appropriate code could be supplied to suit that browser's supported features. This is now considered bad practice and it is now recommended that feature detection be used instead.

For example, querying if the browser supports the useful **addEventListener( )** method determines whether that browser supports the modern Document Object Model.

Hot tip

Previous examples have explicitly used the window prefix to make the parentage of **window** object methods and properties apparent, but it is technically preferable to omit the **window.** prefix – so they are not being referenced via the **window** object's very own **window** property. For example, simply use **onload** rather than **window.onload**.

browser.html

1 Create an HTML document with an empty list
`<ul id="list"></ul>`

2 Next, in a script element, create a self-invoking function that begins by initializing a variable reference
`const list = document.getElementById( 'list' )`

3 Now, add statements to list your browser's names
`list.innerHTML = '<li>Browser: ' + navigator.appName`
`list.innerHTML += '<li>Code Name: ' +`
`                navigator.appCodeName`

4 Then, add statements to list the version details of your browser and of your operating system

```
list.innerHTML += '<li>Version: ' + navigator.appVersion
list.innerHTML += '<li>Platform: ' + navigator.platform
```

5 Finally, add a statement to confirm that you have a modern browser

```
if( window.addEventListener )
{
  list.innerHTML += '<li>This is a modern DOM browser'
}
```

6 Save the HTML document, then open it in any browser to see the name and version details

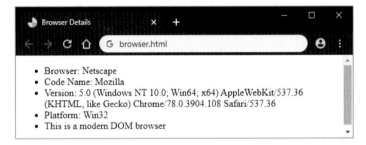

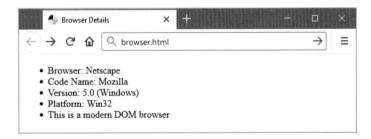

Hot tip

In all modern web browsers, the **window** object has an **addEventListener( )** method – you will discover more about this in Chapter 7, which demonstrates window events.

121

Hot tip

The reason that Google Chrome and other browsers describe themselves as Netscape, Mozilla emanates from the era of the "Browser Wars" – when browsers had to assume those names so they could be served all the web pages that Netscape Mozilla browsers could load.

Check Status

The DOM **window** object's **navigator** child object has a **javaEnabled( )** method that will return **true** only if Java support is enabled in the web browser.

There is also a **cookieEnabled** property that will be **true** only if cookie support is enabled in the browser.

Additionally, **navigator** has a **plugins** child object and a **mimeTypes** child object. As with other arrays, the **plugins** and **mimeTypes** arrays both have a **length** property containing the numeric total of their elements.

Each **plugin** array element has a **name** and **description** property containing details of one installed plugin feature. These can be referenced using the element index number as usual. For example, **navigator.plugins[0].name** references the **name** property of the first element in the **plugins** array.

Similarly, each **mimeTypes** array element has a **type** and **description** property containing details of one supported MIME feature. These can be referenced using the element index number as usual. For example, **navigator.mimeTypes[0].type** references the **type** property of the first element in the **mimeTypes** array.

Don't forget

The contents of these array elements vary according to which features are supported by each browser.

enabled.html

1 Create an HTML document with an empty paragraph
<p id="info"></p>

2 Next, in a script element, create a self-invoking function that begins by initializing two variables
const info = document.getElementById('info')
let status = ''

3 Now, add statements to write a confirmation in the paragraph only if Java support is enabled
status = (navigator.javaEnabled( )) ? 'Enabled' : 'Disabled'
info.innerHTML += 'Java Support is ' + status + '<hr>'

4 Then, add statements to write a confirmation in the paragraph only if cookie support is enabled
status = (navigator.cookieEnabled) ? 'Enabled' : 'Disabled'
info.innerHTML += 'Cookie Support is ' + status + '<hr>'

5 Now, add statements to write the length of the plugins array and an example element

```
if ( navigator.plugins.length !== 0 )
{
  info.innerHTML += 'No. of Plugins: ' +
              navigator.plugins.length
  info.innerHTML += '<br>Example: ' +
              navigator.plugins[ 0 ].name
  info.innerHTML += '<br>For: ' +
              navigator.plugins[ 0 ].description + '<hr>'
}
```

You could use loops to write all **plugins** and **mimeTypes** element contents.

6 Finally, add statements to write the length of the MIME types array and an example element

```
if ( navigator.mimeTypes.length !== 0 )
{
  info.innerHTML += 'No. of MIME Types: ' +
              navigator.mimeTypes.length
  info.innerHTML += '<br>Example: ' +
              navigator.mimeTypes[ 1 ].type
  info.innerHTML += '<br>For: ' +
              navigator.mimeTypes[ 1 ].description
}
```

7 Save the HTML document, then open it in any browser to see the status of its enabled features

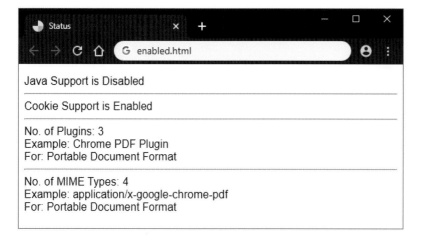

Control Location

The window's **location** object has five properties containing the components of the full URL address of the document currently loaded in the browser window. The complete address, describing the protocol, domain name, file name, and fragment anchor if applicable, is contained in the **location.href** property. Separate components of the complete address are contained in the **location.protocol** (http: or https:), **location.host** (domain name), **location.pathname** (file path), and **location.hash** (fragment anchor). Assigning a new URL to the **location** property will cause the browser to load that page or other resource at that address.

location.html

1 Create an HTML document with a paragraph that contains a hyperlink anchor
```
<p id="info">
<a id="frag">Fragment Anchor</a>
</p>
```

2 Next, in a script element, create a self-invoking function that begins by initializing two variables
```
const info = document.getElementById( 'info' )
let jump = confirm( 'Jump to Fragment?' )
```

3 Now, add a statement to change the window's location if the user has agreed to a request
```
if ( jump )
{
  location = location.href + '#frag'
}
```

Don't forget

A web browser can load a file of any supported MIME type – for example, the MIME type of **image/png for** all PNG image files.

4 Then, add statements to write each component of the current location address in the panel
```
info.innerHTML += '<hr>Href: ' + location.href
info.innerHTML += '<br>Protocol: ' + location.protocol
info.innerHTML += '<br>Host: ' + location.host
info.innerHTML += '<br>Path: ' + location.pathname
info.innerHTML += '<br>Hash: ' + location.hash
```

5 Save the HTML document, then open it in any browser to see a confirm dialog request a change of location

6 Click the Cancel button to deny the request and see the page load at its "root" location, as usual

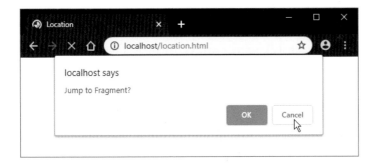

The location shown here is that of the page located on a web server on the local system. If the page was located on your desktop, the protocol would be **file:** and there would be no **host** value.

7 Refresh the browser, then click the OK button to accept the request and see the page load at its fragment location

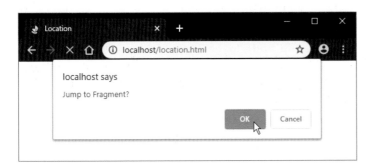

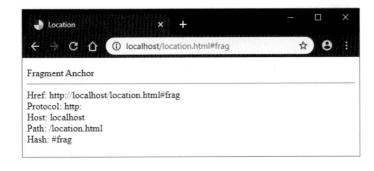

Travel History

The web browser stores a history of the URLs visited in the current session as an array within the **window** object's **history** child object. Like other arrays, this has a **length** property, but also **back( )** and **forward( )** methods to move between elements. Alternatively, the history object's **go( )** method accepts a positive or negative integer argument specifying how many elements to move along the array. For example, **history.go(1)** moves forward one element, and **history.go(-2)** moves back two elements.

page-1.html
page-2.html
page-3.html

1 Create three identical HTML documents that contain an empty paragraph and embed the same external script file

```
<p id="info" > </p>

<script src="history.js" > </script>
```

history.js

2 Next, create the script file with a self-invoking function that begins by initializing a variable reference
const info = document.getElementById('info')

3 Now, in the function block, add statements to write content into the empty paragraphs
```
info.innerHTML +=
  '<a href="page-1.html">Page 1</a> | '
info.innerHTML +=
  '<a href="page-2.html">Page 2</a> | '
info.innerHTML +=
  '<a href="page-3.html">Page 3</a>'
info.innerHTML +=
  '<br>History Length: ' + history.length
info.innerHTML +=
  '<br>Current Location: ' + location.pathname + '<br>'
```

To clear the browser history in the Google Chrome browser, click the ⦂ button, then select **More tools**, **Clear browsing data**, and click the **Clear data** button.

4 Then, add statements to create buttons in the paragraphs
```
info.innerHTML +=
  '<button onclick="history.back( )">Back</button>'
info.innerHTML +=
  '<button onclick="history.forward( )">Forward</button>'
```

5 Save the HTML document and JavaScript script file in the same folder, then clear your browser's history

...cont'd

6 Open the first page to see the initial history length is 1

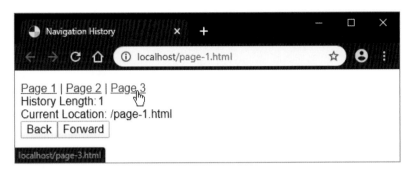

The URLs are stored in the **history** object array elements in a protected manner so they cannot be retrieved as strings.

7 Click a link to load the third page and see the history length increase to 2

8 Click the Back button to return to the first page but see the history length remain the same as 2

In this example, each URL only gets added to the **history** array when moving to a different page by clicking on a link. The **back( )**, **forward( )**, and **go( )** methods simply select an element in the **history** array so do not change its **length** property.

Summary

- The Document Object Model (DOM) is a hierarchical tree representation of all components of a web page.

- The **window** object is the top level in the DOM hierarchy and has properties describing the browser window.

- The **screen** object is a child of the **window** object and has properties describing the screen dimensions and color depth.

- The **window** object has **scrollBy( )** and **scrollTo( )** methods and **scrollX** and **scrollY** properties that specify the scroll position.

- Dialog messages can be displayed using the **window** object's **alert( )**, **confirm( )**, and **prompt( )** methods.

- A pop-up window can be created using the **window** object's **open( )** method, but may be obstructed by a pop-up blocker.

- The **window** object's **setTimeout( )** method creates a timer, which can be canceled later using the **clearTimeout( )** method.

- The **navigator** object is a child of the **window** object and has properties describing the browser and host platform versions.

- The **window** object exists in the global namespace so all its child objects need not include the **window** part of the address.

- Feature detection is used to identify the modern DOM.

- The **navigator.plugins** and **navigator.mimeTypes** properties are arrays that contain details of supported features.

- The **location** object is a child of the **window** object and has properties describing the address of the loaded document.

- The **history** object is a child of the **window** object that contains an array of visited locations in the current session.

- The **history** object has **back( )**, **forward( )**, and **go( )** methods that are used to move through pages in the current session.

7 Interact with the Document

Extract Info

Most interesting of all the DOM **window** object's children is the **document** object, which provides access to the HTML document.

The **document** object has a number of properties describing the document and its location:

- The **document.title** property contains the value specified within the HTML document's title element.

- The location of the HTML document is contained within the **document.URL** property, and is similar to the value contained in the **location.href** property.

- The domain hosting the document is contained in the **document.domain** property, similar to the **location.host** value.

- HTML documents supply the date of their creation or last modification as an HTTP header to the browser so it may decide whether to use a cached copy of the document or seek a new copy. This date can also be retrieved in JavaScript from the DOM's **document.lastModified** property.

- There is a **document.referrer** property that stores the URL of the web page containing the hyperlink that the user followed to load the current HTML document. This is only set if the user followed a hyperlink to load the page, not if they typed in the URL or used some other method to load the page.

info-1.html

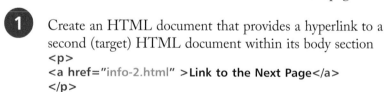
1 Create an HTML document that provides a hyperlink to a second (target) HTML document within its body section
```
<p>
<a href="info-2.html" >Link to the Next Page</a>
</p>
```

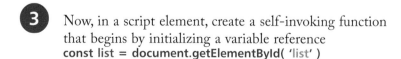

info-2.html

2 Next, create the target HTML document, which contains an empty unordered list
```
<ul id="list"></ul>
```

3 Now, in a script element, create a self-invoking function that begins by initializing a variable reference
```
const list = document.getElementById( 'list' )
```

4 Then, add statements to list features of the document
```
list.innerHTML = '<li>Linked From: ' + document.referrer
list.innerHTML += '<li>Title: ' + document.title
list.innerHTML += '<li>URL: ' + document.URL
list.innerHTML += '<li>Domain: ' + document.domain
list.innerHTML += '<li>Last Modified: ' +
                                 document.lastModified
```

5 Save the HTML documents in the same folder, then open the document containing the link in your browser

6 Now, click on the hyperlink to load the second HTML document in the browser and see document information

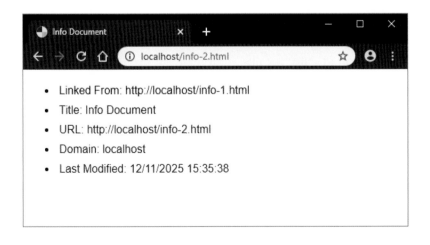

The date contained in **document.lastModified** only relates to the HTML document itself, not to any external style sheets or external script files that the HTML document may import.

The domain shown here is that of the page located on a web server on the local system. If the page was located on your desktop, the **document.referrer** and **document.domain** properties would not be set with any values.

Address Arrays

The DOM **document** object has child objects of **forms**, **images**, **links**, **styleSheets**, and **scripts**. Each of these children is an array in which every array element represents a document component in the same order they appear within the HTML document. For example, the first image in the document body, specified by an HTML **<img>** tag, is represented by **document.images[0]**. This means its URL can be referenced using **document.images[0].src**, which reveals the path assigned to the **src** attribute of the HTML **<img>** tag. Assigning this component a new URL in a script will dynamically replace the old image with a different image.

The **links** array represents HTML **<a>** tags within the HTML document; the **styleSheets** array represents HTML **<style>** tags; and the **scripts** array represents HTML **<script>** tags.

The **forms** array represents HTML **<form>** tags but also has its own child **elements** object that is an array of all the form components. For example, the value of the first component of the first form in an HTML document can be referenced using **document.forms[0].elements[0].value**. Assigning this component a new value in a script will dynamically replace the old value.

Beware

Notice the "camelCase" capitalization of the **styleSheets** array.

components.html

① Create an HTML document containing a form and an empty list
```
<form>
<img src="user.png" alt="User" height="64" width="64" >
<input type="text" name="topic" size="30"
                value="Type Your Question Here" >
<input type="button" value="Ask a Question" > <br>
<a href="formhelp.html" style="margin:5px">Help?</a>
</form>

<ul id="list"></ul>
```

② Now, add a style sheet to style the font and form
```
< style>
* { font : 1em sans-serif ; }
form { width : 500px ; height : 100px ;
                background : url(bg.png) ; }
</style>
```

user.png
64px x 64px
(gray areas are transparent)

bg.png
24px x
100px

③ Next, in a script element, create a self-invoking function that begins by initializing a variable reference
```
const list = document.getElementById( 'list' )
```

4 Now, add statements to list components of the document
```
list.innerHTML = '<li>No. Forms: ' +
                        document.forms.length
list.innerHTML += '<li>No. Links: ' +
                        document.links.length
list.innerHTML += '<li>No. Images: ' +
                        document.images.length
list.innerHTML += '<li>No. Style Sheets: ' +
                        document.styleSheets.length
list.innerHTML += '<li>No. Scripts: ' +
                        document.scripts.length
```

5 Finally, add statements to list two attribute values
```
list.innerHTML += '<li>First Image URL: ' +
                        document.images[ 0 ].src
list.innerHTML += '<li>First Form Element Value: ' +
                        document.forms[ 0 ].elements[ 0 ].value
```

6 Save the HTML document, then open it in your browser to see components of the document listed

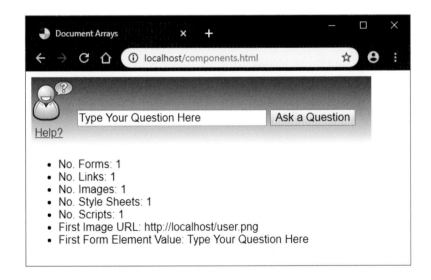

The array elements only represent the relevant HTML tags.

Notice that images incorporated within a document by style rules are not included in the **images** array, only those that are incorporated by HTML **<img>** tags – so here the form background image (**bg.png**) does not appear in the **images** array. Similarly, the style rule assigned inline to the **style** attribute is not included in the **styleSheets** array.

Address Elements

Using the component arrays with dot notation to reference a specific element requires the script author to count the number of components to calculate each index position. This is especially tedious with lengthy documents, is error-prone, and modification of the HTML document can change the element's index position. This was required in earlier years but was eventually resolved by the addition of three new methods to the **document** object:

● The **document.getElementById( )** method, used by previous examples in this book to add content from JavaScript code, allows any component to be referenced by its HTML **id** attribute value. This method simply specifies the target **id** value as its argument and is used to reference a single specific HTML element.

● The **document.getElementsByTagName( )** method returns an array-like **HTMLCollection** object that references all HTML elements of the tag name specified as its argument. A specific HTML element can then be referenced using its element index number, as you would do in an array.

● The **document.getElementsByClassName( )** method returns an array-like **HTMLCollection** object that references all HTML elements containing a **class** attribute that has been assigned the name specified as its argument. A specific HTML element can then be referenced using its element index number, as you would do in an array.

Beware

In the name of the two methods that return an **HTMLCollection** it's "Elements" (plural) but in the name of the other method it's "Element" (singular).

collection.html

1 Create an HTML document containing two lists and an empty paragraph
```
<ol>
<li class="fruit">Apple</li>
<li class="nut">Almond</li>
<li class="fruit">Apricot</li>
</ol>

<ol>
<li class="fruit">Blackberry</li>
<li id="country" class="nut">Brazil</li>
<li class="fruit">Banana</li>
</ol>

<p id="info"></p>
```

2 Next, in a script element, create a self-invoking function that begins by initializing five variables

```
const info = document.getElementById( 'info' )
const item = document.getElementById( 'country' )
const lists = document.getElementsByTagName( 'ol' )
const fruits = document.getElementsByClassName( 'fruit' )
let i = 0
```

3 Now, add a statement to describe an element object and the text that element contains

```
info.innerHTML = item + ' Id: ' + item.innerText + '<br>'
```

4 Then, add statements to describe an **HTMLCollection** object and the text its elements contain

```
info.innerHTML += '<br>' + lists + ' Tags:<br>'
for( i = 0; i < lists.length ; i++ ) {
  info.innerHTML += ( i + 1 ) + ' of ' + lists.length
  info.innerHTML += ' : ' + lists[ i ].innerText + '<br>'
}
```

Hot tip

The **innerText** property of an element returns only the content between its opening and closing tags, whereas the **innerHTML** property also returns the HTML tags. Change this to **innerHTML** to see the difference.

5 Finally, add statements to describe a second **HTMLCollection** object and the text its elements contain

```
info.innerHTML += '<br>' + fruits + ' Class:<br>'
for( i = 0 ; i < fruits.length ; i++ ) {
  info.innerHTML += ( i + 1 ) + ' of ' + fruits.length
  info.innerHTML += ' : ' + fruits[ i ].innerText+ '<br>'
}
```

6 Save the HTML document, then open it in your browser to see the element values retrieved by different methods

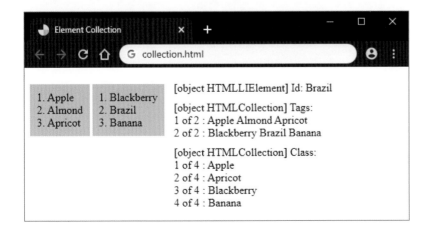

Write Content

As witnessed in previous examples, the **innerHTML** and **innerText** properties of the **document** object can be used to write content into existing elements. The **document** object also has a **write( )** method that provides another way to write content, but this automatically calls a **document.open( )** method to start a new document – so the current document is no longer displayed.

More usefully, a **document.createElement( )** method accepts a tag name as its argument and creates an element of that type. Content can then be added to the new element by assignment to its **innerHTML** or **innerText** properties. It can then be inserted into the web page within an existing element by specifying the new element as the argument to a **document.appendChild( )** method.

You can also dynamically write attributes into elements by specifying an attribute name and value as two arguments to an element's **setAttribute( )** method.

write.html

1 Create an HTML document that contains a heading and an ordered list of three items
```
<h1 id="heading">Top 3 Cities</h1>
<ol id="list">
<li>Tokyo, Japan
<li>New York, USA
<li>Rio de Janeiro, Brazil
</ol>
```

2 Save the HTML document, then open it in your browser to see the web page

3 Next, in a script element, create a self-invoking function that begins by initializing two variables as new list item elements and one variable reference
```
const itemFour = document.createElement( 'li' )
const itemFive = document.createElement( 'li' )
const heading = document.getElementById( 'heading' )
```

4 Now, assign text content to the two new elements
```
itemFour.innerText = 'London, England'
itemFive.innerText = 'Cape Town, South Africa'
```

5 Then, insert the new element content into the web page as children of the ordered list element
```
document.getElementById( 'list' ).appendChild( itemFour )
document.getElementById( 'list' ).appendChild( itemFive )
```

6 Add an attribute to the existing heading element to change its font color
```
heading.setAttribute( 'style', 'color:Red' )
```

7 Finally, change the heading to better describe the extended list
```
heading.innerText = 'Best Five Cities'
```

8 Save the HTML document once more, then refresh your browser to see the newly written content

Hot tip

An existing element may be removed from the web page by specifying it as the argument to a **document.removeChild( )** method, or replaced by specifying new and old elements as arguments to a **document.replaceChild( )** method.

Hot tip

You can remove an attribute by specifying the attribute's name as the argument to an element's **removeAttribute( )** method.

Manage Cookies

For security reasons JavaScript cannot write regular files on the user's hard drive, but it can write "cookie" files to store a small amount of data. These are limited in size to a maximum of 4KB and in number to 20 per web server. Typically, the data stored in a cookie will identify the user for subsequent visits to a website.

Cookie data is stored in the DOM **document** object's **cookie** property as one or more "key=value" pairs, terminated with a ";" semicolon character. The value may not contain whitespace, commas, or semi-colons, unless passed as the argument to the built-in **encodeURI( )** function, which encodes the string in Unicode format – for example, this represents a space as **%20**.

By default, the lifespan of a cookie is limited to the current browser session unless an expiry date is specified when the cookie is created as an "expires=date" pair, in which the date value is a UTC string. Typically, this is achieved using a JavaScript **Date** object converted with its **toUTCString( )** method. Setting an existing cookie's expiry date to a past time will delete that cookie.

Retrieving data from a cookie requires some string manipulation to return Unicode to regular text, using the built-in **decodeURI( )** function so **%20** becomes a space character once more, and to separate the name and value items of data. Within the cookie string multiple pairs can be separated by specifying the ";" semicolon as the argument to the **split( )** method. Similarly, keys and values can be separated by specifying the "=" character as the argument to the **split( )** method. Likewise, where the value is a comma-separated list of items, the "," comma can be specified as the argument to the **split( )** method to separate them as array elements.

It is useful to create an external JavaScript file containing "setter" and "getter" utility functions that can easily be called to store and retrieve cookie data.

Beware

The cookie expiry date cannot normally be read by JavaScript. If it is required to be readable, also add it to the list of cookie values.

Hot tip

The long number used to set the expiry here is the number of milliseconds in one day.

cookie.js

1 Begin a JavaScript file with a setter function that has parameters for key, value, and expiry arguments

```
function setCookie( key, value, days ) {
  const d = new Date( )
  d.setTime( d.getTime( ) + ( days * 86400000 )  )
  document.cookie = key + '=' + encodeURI( value ) +
                       ';expires=' + d.toUTCString( ) + ';'
}
```

2 Then, add a getter function to accept a key argument

```javascript
function getCookie( key ) {
  if( document.cookie )
  {
    const pairs = decodeURI( document.cookie ).split( ';' )
    let i, name, value
    for( i = 0 ; i < pairs.length ; i++ )
    {
      name = ( pairs[ i ].split( '=' )[ 0 ] ).trim( )
      if( name === key ) { value = pairs[ i ].split( '=' )[ 1 ] }
    }
    return value
  }
}
```

Beware

Notice that the **trim( )** method is used here to remove any whitespace from the ends of the name.

3 Next, create an HTML document that contains an empty list and imports the external JavaScript file

```html
<ul id="list"></ul> <script src="cookie.js"></script>
```

cookie.html

4 Now, in another script element, create a self-invoking function that sets a cookie, then gets its values

```javascript
setCookie( 'User','Mike McGrath,12345', 7 )

const list = document.getElementById( 'list' )
let i, value = getCookie( 'User' )
if( value.indexOf( ',' ) )
{
  value = value.split( ',' )
}
for( i = 0 ; i < value.length ; i++ )
{
  list.innerHTML += '<li>' + value[ i ]
}
```

Don't forget

A cookie may be deleted by setting its expiry date to a date prior to the current actual date.

5 Save the HTML document and JavaScript file in the same folder on a web server, then open the web page in your browser to see the retrieved cookie values

Cookies   ×   +

← → C ⌂ ⓘ localhost/cookie.html ☆ 😀 ⋮

- Mike McGrath
- 12345

Load Events

The DOM allows JavaScript to react to "events" that occur on a web page by the script author providing functions that will be executed when a particular event happens. These functions are known as "event-handlers", and can react to events such as:

- **load** – fires when the page has loaded into the browser
- **click** – fires when the user clicks a mouse button
- **keydown** – fires when the user presses a keyboard key
- **change** – fires when the user modifies an input field
- **submit** – fires when the user submits an HTML form

To react to a load event, an event-handler function name can be nominated by assignment to the **window** object's **onload** property, using this syntax:

onload= *function-name*

Alternatively, the event name and the event-handler function name can be specified as arguments to the **window** object's **addEventListener( )** method, but the event name must be enclosed within quotes, like this:

addEventListener('load' , *function-name* **)**

An event-handler for the load event might be used to examine the browser's features, and can usefully check for cookie data.

Hot tip

There is also an unload event that fires when the user leaves the page. Its event-handler can be nominated by assignment to the **window.onunload** property, or can be specified to the **addEventListener( )** method.

HTML

load.html

1 Create an HTML document that contains a paragraph with a link to the cookies example on pages 138-139, an empty paragraph, and imports the external JavaScript file from the previous example
```
<p><a href="cookie.html">Link</a></p>
<p id="info"></p>
<script src="cookie.js"></script>
```

2 Next, in a script element, nominate an event-handler function to be executed when the page has loaded
```
addEventListener( 'load', welcome )
```

3 Now, add the event-handler function to greet the user

```
function welcome( ) {
  const info = document.getElementById( 'info' )
  if( getCookie( 'Name' ) )
  {
    info.innerHTML = 'Welcome Back, ' + getCookie( 'Name' )
  }
  else
  {
    let name = prompt( 'Please Enter Your Name', 'User' )
    setCookie( 'Name', name, 7 )
    info.innerHTML = 'Welcome, ' + name
  }
}
```

The second argument to the **prompt( )** method is the default input value.

4 Save the HTML document and open it in your browser, – enter your name, follow the link, then click the back button

localhost says

Please Enter Your Name

John Smith

OK   Cancel

Mouse Events

Event-handler functions that execute when the user clicks on a particular object in the HTML document can be nominated by assigning the function name to the object's **onclick** and **ondblclick** properties. These respond to the "click" event that fires when the user clicks the mouse button once, and the "dblclick" event that fires when the mouse button is pressed twice in quick succession.

Additionally, an object's **onmousedown** and **onmouseup** properties can nominate event-handler functions to execute when the mouse button gets pressed down, firing the "mousedown" event, and when it gets released, firing the "mouseup" event.

Similarly, an object's **onmouseover** and **onmouseout** properties can nominate event-handler functions to execute when the mouse is placed over an element, firing the "mouseover" event, and when it moves off the element, firing the "mouseout" event. These are often used to create a rollover effect, such as changing the value of that element's **style.background** property to a different color value.

Alternatively, the event name and the event-handler function name can be specified as arguments to that object's **addEventListener( )** method. This can be used just like the **window** object's **addEventListener( )** method in the previous example to nominate a function by name, or you can write a function definition inline as the second argument.

When an event occurs, an **event** object can be passed to an inline event-handler function. This has a **type** property that identifies the name of that event.

mouse.html

1 Create an HTML document that contains two paragraphs and a button
```
<p id="box">Target</p>
<p id="info">Place Mouse Over Target</p>
<button id="btn">Click Me</button>
```

2 Next, in a script element, create a self-invoking function that begins by initializing two variables
```
( function ( ) {
  const box = document.getElementById( 'box' )
  const btn = document.getElementById( 'btn' )

  // Statements to be inserted here.
} ) ( )
```

3 Now, insert statements to nominate inline event-handlers that will pass arguments to a second function

```
box.addEventListener( 'mouseover',
        function ( event ) { reactTo( event, 'Red' ) } )
box.addEventListener( 'mouseout',
        function ( event ) { reactTo( event, 'Purple' ) } )
box.addEventListener( 'mousedown',
        function ( event ) { reactTo( event, 'Green' ) } )
box.addEventListener( 'mouseup',
        function ( event ) { reactTo( event, 'Blue' ) } )
btn.addEventListener( 'click',
        function ( event ) { reactTo( event, 'Orange' ) } )
```

If removing an object that has event-handlers attached, you should also remove its event-handlers to avoid creating memory leaks.

4 Finally, add a second function to display the event type and change the first paragraph's background color

```
function reactTo( event, color ) {
  document.getElementById( 'box' ).style.background = color
  document.getElementById( 'info' ).innerText = event.type
}
```

5 Save the HTML document and open it in your browser, then use your mouse to see the events and reactions

143

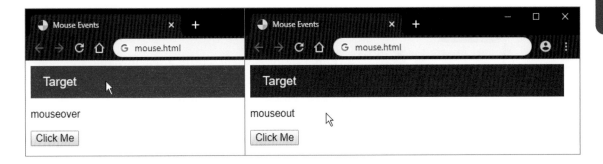

Event Values

In addition to the mouse events described on pages 142-143, there is a "mousemove" event. This can pass an **event** object to an event-handler function with **x** and **y** properties that contain the current window coordinates of the mouse pointer.

There is also a "keydown" event that fires when the user first presses a key, a "keypress" event that fires when the key is pressed down, and a "keyup" event that fires when the key is released. These can each pass an **event** object to an event-handler function with a **type** property that identifies the name of that event, and a **keyCode** property that stores the numerical value of the last key pressed.

The numerical value of a key is its Unicode value, which can be specified as the argument to a **String.fromCharCode( )** method to translate it to a character value.

Event-handler functions can be nominated to **onmousemove**, **onkeydown**, **onkeypress**, and **onkeyup** properties, or be specified as arguments to an object's **addEventListener( )** method.

Hot tip

Unicode values for common characters are the same as ASCII code values, where lowercase a-z is 65-90 and A-Z is 97-122.

HTML

values.html

1 Create an HTML document that contains an empty paragraph
```
<p id="info"></p>
```

2 Next, in a script element, create a self-invoking function that nominates an event-handler function for three events and passes an event argument to that function
```
( function ( ) {
  document.addEventListener( 'keydown',
            function ( event ){ reactTo( event ) } )
  document.addEventListener( 'keyup',
            function ( event ){ reactTo( event ) } )
  document.addEventListener( 'mousemove',
            function ( event ){ reactTo( event ) } )
} ) ( )
```

3 Now, begin the event-handler function with a statement to initialize a variable
```
function reactTo( event ) {

  const info = document.getElementById( 'info' )

  // Statements to be inserted here.
}
```

4 Then, insert statements to display the current window coordinate values of the mouse pointer

```
if( event.type === 'mousemove' )
{
  info.innerHTML =
  'Mouse pointer is at X:' + event.x + ' Y:' + event.y
}
```

5 Next, add statements to display the Unicode value of a keyboard key when pressed

```
if( event.type === 'keydown' )
{
  info.innerHTML += '<hr>' + event.type
  info.innerHTML += ': ' + event.keyCode
}
```

6 Finally, add statements to display the character of that keyboard key when released

```
if( event.type === 'keyup' )
{
  info.innerHTML += '<br>' + event.type + ': ' +
        String.fromCharCode( event.keyCode ) + '<hr>'
}
```

7 Save the HTML document then open it in your browser and move the mouse pointer over the window to see its displayed coordinate values change as the mouse moves

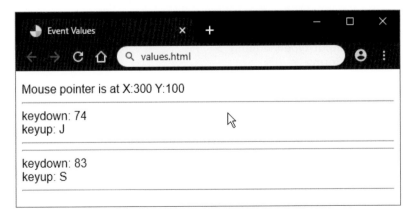

8 Press any alphanumeric keyboard key to see that key's Unicode number and character value

Check Boxes

Radio button groups allow the user to select any one button from the group, and the HTML name attributes of all radio button input elements in that group share the same name. In scripting terms, that group name is the name of an array in which each radio button object can be referenced using its array index value.

Unlike radio button groups, checkbox button groups allow the user to select one or more buttons in that group. But as with radio button groups, each name attribute shares the same group name. That group name is also the name of an array in which each checkbox button object can be referenced by its array index value.

Both radio button objects and checkbox button objects have a **checked** Boolean property, which is **true** when the button is selected and **false** otherwise. Looping through a button group array to inspect the **checked** property of each object determines which buttons are selected. A script statement can also assign a **true** value to the **checked** property of a button to select it.

checkbox.html

1 Create an HTML document that contains a form with a group of three checkboxes and a submit button

```
<form id="pizza" action="echo.pl" method="POST">
<fieldset>
<legend>Select Pizza Toppings</legend>
<input type="checkbox" name="Top"
                          value="Cheese">Cheese
<input type="checkbox" name="Top"
                          value="Ham">Ham
<input type="checkbox" name="Top"
                          value="Peppers">Peppers
</fieldset>
<input type="submit">
</form>
```

2 Next, in a script element, create a self-invoking function that nominates an event-handler function for the form's "submit" event and checks one checkbox

```
( function ( ) {

  const form = document.getElementById( 'pizza' )
  form.addEventListener( 'submit',
        function ( event ) { reactTo( form, event ) } )
  form.Top[ 0 ].checked = true

} ) ( )
```

Hot tip

When multiple buttons in a checkbox button group have been selected, their values are submitted as a comma-separated list.

3 Now, begin the event-handler function by declaring three variables and a loop to determine which boxes are checked

```
function reactTo( form, event ) {
  let i, ok, summary = ''

  for( i = 0 ; i < form.Top.length ; i++ )
  {
    if( form.Top[ i ].checked )
    {
      summary += form.Top[ i ].value + ' '
    }
  }

  // Statements to be inserted here.
}
```

4 Then, add statements to confirm the choices and submit them to the web server, or cancel the submission

```
ok = confirm( 'Submit These Choices?\n' + summary )
if( !ok ) { event.preventDefault( ) }
```

5 Save the HTML document on a web server then open it in a browser, make your choices, then confirm submission

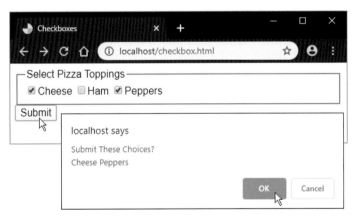

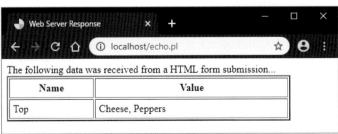

Hot tip

When a form button gets clicked it triggers the form's default **event** action, which is to submit the form data to the web server. Calling the form event's **preventDefault( )** method stops the form data submission.

Don't forget

This example is run on a local web server that supports the PERL server-side script that processes the form submission and provides the response to the web browser.

echo.pl

Select Options

Options presented in an HTML **<select>** drop-down list object are uniquely represented in the DOM by an **options[ ]** array, in which each array element contains the option specified by an HTML **<option>** tag. Upon submission to the web server, the value assigned to the **name** attribute of the **<select>** tag, and that assigned to the **value** attribute of the currently selected **<option>** tag are sent as a name=value pair.

Importantly, the selection list object has a **selectedIndex** property, which contains the index number of the currently selected **options[ ]** array element, and this can be used to retrieve the value of the current selected option.

When the user changes the selected option in a selection list, a "change" event fires. The list object's **onchange** property can nominate an event-handler function to execute when the selected option changes. Alternatively, the event name and the event-handler function name can be specified as arguments to the list object's **addEventListener( )** method.

options.html

Notice that the HTML **selected** attribute selects the first option element, which is represented in the DOM by **options[0]**

1 Create an HTML document that contains a form selection list and a submit button, plus an empty paragraph

```
<form action="echo.pl" method="POST">
<select id="list" name="City">
<option value="Rome" selected>Rome</option>
<option value="London">London</option>
<option value="New York" >New York</option>
</select>
<input type="submit">
</form>

<p id="info"></p>
```

2 Next, in a script element, create a self-invoking function that nominates an event-handler function for the form's "submit" event and for the window's "load" event

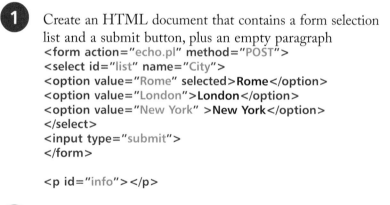

```
( function ( ) {

   const list = document.getElementById( 'list' )
   list.addEventListener( 'change' ,
              function ( ) { reactTo( list, event ) } )
   addEventListener( 'load' ,
              function ( ) { reactTo( list, event ) } )

} ) ( )
```

...cont'd

3 Now, add the event-handler function, which will display the event and current list selection in the paragraph

```
function reactTo( list, event ) {

    const info = document.getElementById( 'info' )
    let index = list.options.selectedIndex
    let city = list.options[ index ].value
    info.innerHTML = event.type + '<br>Selected: '
    info.innerHTML += city + '<br>Index: ' + index
}
```

Hierarchically, this selected option can be referenced using **document.forms[0]. elements[0].options[1]. value** – the deepest level of the DOM.

4 Save the HTML document on a web server then open it in a browser, select an option, and submit the form

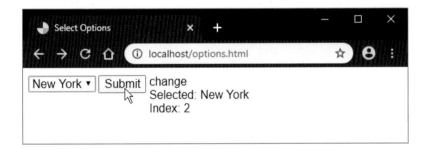

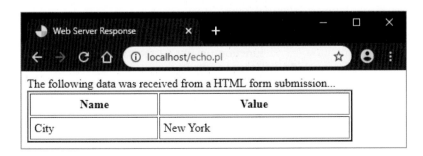

echo.pl

Reset Changes

An event-handler can be nominated to the **onfocus** and **onfocusout** properties of form text input objects and textarea objects to recognize the active element. A "focus" event fires when the user selects a text field, and a "focusout" event fires when the user leaves that text field.

Usefully, an event-handler can be nominated to the **onreset** property of a form object to remove content related to form input when the form is returned to its original state by a reset button.

As with other objects, the event name and the event-handler function name can be specified as arguments to the text field and form object's **addEventListener( )** method.

reset.html

Hot tip

Text fields also have an **onselect** property to which an event-handler can be nominated to respond to a "select" event that fires when the user selects some of its text.

1 Create an HTML document that contains a form with a text field and reset button, plus an empty paragraph

```
<form id="code" >
<input id="lang" name="Language" type="text" >
<input type="reset">
<input type="submit">
</form>

<p id="info"></p>
```

2 Next, in a script element, create a self-invoking function that nominates an event-handler function for the text field's "focus" and "focusout" events, the form's "reset" event, and for the window's "load" event

```
( function ( ) {

const form = document.getElementById( 'code' )
const lang = document.getElementById( 'lang' )
const info = document.getElementById( 'info' )

lang.addEventListener( 'focus' ,
                function ( event ) { reactTo( event, info ) } )
lang.addEventListener( 'focusout' ,
                function ( event ) { reactTo( event, info ) } )
form.addEventListener( 'reset',
                function ( ) { defaultMessage( info ) } )
addEventListener( 'load',
                function ( ) { defaultMessage( info ) } )

} ) ( )
```

3 Now, add the event-handler function for the text field's "focus" and "focusout" events, to display the event type

```
function reactTo( event, info ) {
  info.innerHTML = event.type
}
```

4 Then, add the event-handler function for the window's "load" and the form's "reset" events, to display a message

```
function defaultMessage( info ) {
  info.innerHTML =
        'Please enter your favorite coding language'
}
```

5 Save the HTML document, then open it in your browser, to see the default message appear in the paragraph

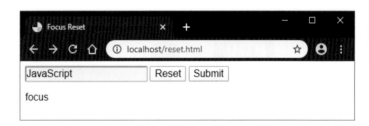

6 Select the text field and see the "focus" event fire, then type in the name of your favorite coding language

7 Hit the Tab key to move focus onto the Reset button and see the "focusout" event fire

8 Hit the Enter key (to push the Reset button) to clear the text field and see the default message once more

Validate Forms

A form object's **onsubmit** property can nominate an event-handler function to validate user input entered into a form before it is submitted to the web server for processing. Alternatively, the "submit" event name and an event-handler function name can be specified as arguments to the form object's **addEventListener( )** method.

The simplest level of form validation examines a text input where an entry is required to ensure the user has made an entry. When its value remains an empty string, no entry has been made, so the validating function can call the **event.preventDefault( )** method to prevent form submission.

A higher level of form validation can examine the string entered by the user to ensure it meets an expected format. For example, where an email address is expected, the format requires the string to contain an "@" character and at least one "." character. When either of these are absent, the string is not a valid email address, so the validating function can prevent form submission.

A form element can be referenced by quoting its **name** attribute value in the form's **elements[ ]** array brackets.

validate.html

1 Create an HTML document that contains a form with two text fields and a submit button

```
<form id="contact" action="echo.pl" method="POST">
<fieldset>
<legend>Please Enter Your Details</legend>
Name: <input type="text" name="Name" value="">
<br><br>
Email: <input type="text" name="Email" value="">
</fieldset>
<input type="submit">
</form>
```

2 Next, in a script element, create a self-invoking function that nominates an event-handler function for the form's "submit" event

```
( function ( ) {

    const form = document.getElementById( 'contact' )

    form.addEventListener( 'submit' ,
        function ( event ) { validate( form, event ) } )
} ) ( )
```

3 Now, add the event-handler function to validate input

```
function validate( form, event ) {
  let value = form.elements[ 'Name' ].value
  if( value === '' ) {
    alert( 'Please Enter Your Name' )
    event.preventDefault( ) ; return }

  value = form.elements[ 'Email' ].value
  if( ( value === '' ) || ( value.indexOf('@') === -1 ) ||
  ( value.indexOf('.') === -1 ) ) {
    alert( 'Please Enter A Valid Email Address' )
    event.preventDefault( ) }
}
```

The **indexOf( )** method returns an integer that is the character position in the string, or -1 if the character is not found. For details see page 102.

4 Save the HTML document on a web server, then open it in a browser, enter your details, and submit the form

echo.pl

Summary

- The **document** object has **title, URL, domain, lastModified,** and **referrer** properties that describe that document.

- The **document** object has **forms, images, links, styleSheets,** and **scripts** child objects that are arrays of document components.

- The **forms** array represents **<form>** tags and has an **elements** child object that is an array of form components.

- The **document** object has **getElementById( )**, **getElementsByTagName( )**, and **getElementsByClassName( )** methods that can be used to reference HTML elements.

- The **innerHTML** and **innerText** properties of the **document** object can be used to write content into existing elements.

- The **document** object has **createElement( )**, **appendChild( )**, and **setAttribute( )** methods that can add content to a document.

- The **document** object's **cookie** property has "key=value" pairs that can store a small amount of data on the user's system.

- The **encodeURI( )**, **decodeURI( )**, **toUTCString( )**, and **split( )** functions are used for string manipulation with cookie data.

- The DOM allows JavaScript to react to events such as **load, click, keydown, change,** and **submit** in response to user actions.

- Event-handler functions can be assigned to an object property or specified by the **addEventListener( )** method.

- An **event** object can be passed to an event-handler function and the event can be identified by its **event.type** property.

- The mousemove **event** object has **x** and **y** properties that contain the current window coordinates of the pointer.

- Radio and checkbox button objects have a **checked** Boolean property, which is only **true** when the button is selected.

- A selection list object has a **selectedIndex** property, which contains the index number of the currently selected **options[ ]** array element.

- The form submit event has a **preventDefault( )** method that can be called to stop submission of a form to the web server.

8 Create Web Applications

Meet JSON

JavaScript Object Notation ("JSON") is a popular text format that is used to store and exchange data. It is a subset of the JavaScript language in which data is stored as a comma-separated list of key:value pairs within a JSON object. All keys must be of the String data type, enclosed in double quote marks, and their associated values may only be one of these data types:

- **String** – enclosed within double quotes, not single quotes.

- **Number** – either integer or floating point.

- **Object** – a JSON object.

- **Array** – but not a Function or a Date.

- **Boolean** – either true or false.

- **null** – but not undefined.

JSON key:value pairs are enclosed in curly brackets, like this:

{"name":"Alice","age":21,"city":"New York"}

You can easily convert a JavaScript object to a JSON object by specifying it as the argument to a **JSON.stringify( )** method.

Conversely, you can convert a JSON object to a JavaScript object by specifying it as the argument to a **JSON.parse( )** method.

Typically, JSON objects store data in a text file with a **.json** file extension as an online resource. A web page script may, therefore, receive data in JSON format from a web server.

After converting a JSON object to a JavaScript object, with the **JSON.parse( )** method, the data can be addressed as usual with dot notation, or with bracket notation.

Both JSON and XML (eXtensible Markup Language) can be used to receive data from a web server, but JSON is considered better because you need to loop through the elements to extract data from the XML format, whereas the **JSON.parse( )** method simply returns a string of all the data.

Usefully, JavaScript can fetch data from online JSON resources for use in web applications.

Hot tip

You can find a free JSON object validator online at jsonlint.com

1 Begin a script with a self-invoking function that creates a JavaScript object containing a String and an Array
```
let obj = { category : 'Fashion' ,
    models : [ { name : 'Alice', age : 21, city : 'New York' } ,
               { name : 'Kelly', age : 23, city : 'Las Vegas' } ] }
```

json.html

2 Next, create a JSON version of the JavaScript object and print it out
```
let json_obj = JSON.stringify( obj )
console.log( json_obj )
```

3 Now, create a JavaScript version of the JSON object and print it out for comparison
```
let new_obj = JSON.parse( json_obj )
console.log( new_obj )
```

4 Finally, print out selected values using both dot notation and bracket notation
```
console.log( new_obj[ 'category' ] )
console.log( new_obj.models[ 0 ].name )
console.log( new_obj[ 'models' ][ 1 ][ 'name' ] )
```

Hot tip

See that the JSON object has all String values within double quotes.

5 Save the HTML document then open it in a web browser and launch the Console in Developer Tools to compare the objects

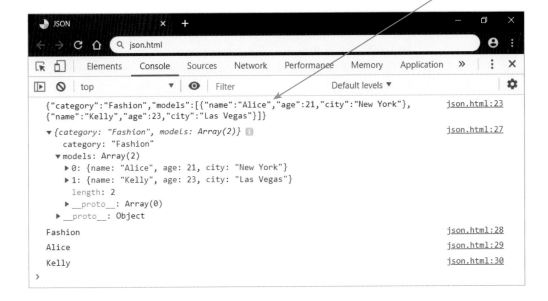

157

Make Promises

JavaScript is a single-threaded "synchronous" language. This means that only one operation can be executed at any given time. As the script proceeds, each operation is added to a "call stack", then executed (in top-down order) – then removed from the stack.

There are, however, some functions that are handled by a browser API ("Application Programming Interface"), rather than by the JavaScript engine. For example, the **setTimeout( )** method is handled by the browser – so that other operations can be executed while waiting for the timer to end. When the timer does end it passes the operation to a "callback queue", then (when it reaches the front of the queue) it gets executed. This entire process is controlled by an "event loop" that constantly monitors the state of the call stack and callback queue.

Hot tip

Web browsers have several APIs, including the Fetch API, which is used to grab resources over a network.

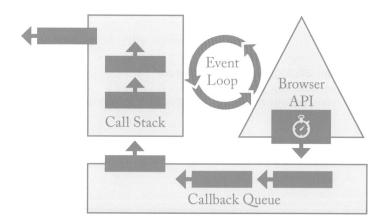

In JavaScript, a **Promise** object represents the eventual completion, or failure, of an asynchronous operation and its resulting value. Its status may be either pending, resolved (completed), or rejected (failed).

Hot tip

You can chain several **then( )** method calls onto a promise, but only one will receive the resolved result.

You create a promise using the JavaScript **new** keyword and the **Promise( )** constructor. This accepts a function as its argument, which in turn accepts the names of two functions that specify what to do when the promise is resolved or rejected.

Each JavaScript promise has **then( )** and **catch( )** methods that can be "chained" after the promise object using dot notation. The **then( )** method can handle the resulting value of the asynchronous operation, and the **catch( )** method can handle errors if rejected.

1 Begin a script with a self-invoking function that creates a JavaScript **Promise** object that will execute one of two functions after a one-second delay

promise.html

```
const promise = new Promise( function( resolve, reject ) {
  let random = Math.round( Math.random( ) * 10 )

  if ( random % 2 === 0 )
  { setTimeout( function( ) { resolve( random ) }, 1000 ) }
  else
  { setTimeout( function( ) { reject( random ) }, 1000 ) }
} )
```

2 Next, add a statement with chained methods that display the promise status and handle the returned values

```
promise
  .then( console.log( promise ) )
  .then( function( res ) { console.log( res + ' Is Even' ) } )
  .catch( function( err )  { console.log( err + ' Is Odd' ) } )
```

3 Save the HTML document then open it in a web browser and launch the Console in Developer Tools to see the asynchronous operations

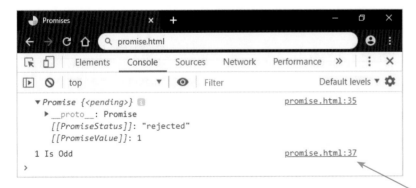

Hot tip

Notice how the Console provides the line number of the promise and of the function that handled the result.

Fetch Data

Web browsers support a Fetch API that can be used in JavaScript to grab resources over a network. The **fetch( )** method accepts a single argument, which is the URL of the resource to be grabbed.

The **fetch( )** method is asynchronous, so that means other operations can be executed while waiting for the resource to arrive. On completion, the **fetch( )** method returns a **Promise** object, which contains a response (an **HTTPResponse** object).

Typically, the **fetch( )** method can grab a JSON resource and parse it using a **json( )** method of the **HTTPResponse** object. The returned JSON data can then be passed as an argument to the next chained promise method, which can in turn pass the JSON data to a handler function. The syntax of the process looks like this:

```
fetch( url )
.then( function( response ) { return response.json( ) } )
.then( function( data ) { return handler( data ) } )
.catch( function( err ) { return console.log( err ) } )
```

Arrow Function Expressions

The function definitions above can, optionally, be written more concisely as JavaScript => arrow function expressions. This allows you to omit the **function** keyword, like this:

```
.then( ( response ) => { return response.json( ) } )
```

If the function body contains only one statement, and that statement returns a value, you can also omit the curly brackets and the **return** keyword from the => arrow function, like this:

```
.then( ( response ) => response.json( ) )
```

Any parameters can appear as a comma-separated list within the round ( ) brackets, as usual, but if there is only one parameter you can even omit the brackets from the => arrow function – so the entire syntax of the process can, optionally, look like this:

```
fetch( url )
.then( response => response.json( ) )
.then( data => handler( data ) )
.catch( err => console.log( err ) )
```

This is more readable, but you should be aware that => arrow functions treat the **this** keyword differently to regular functions.

Beware

With arrow functions, the **this** keyword represents the object in the originating context, whereas with regular functions, the **this** keyword represents the object that calls the function.

1 Open a plain text editor, such as Windows' Notepad app, then create a JSON document with an object containing five key:value pairs

weekdays.json

```
weekdays.json - Notepad                          —    □    ×
File  Edit  Format  View  Help
{
  "DAY1":"Monday", "DAY2":"Tuesday", "DAY3":"Wednesday",
  "DAY4":"Thursday", "DAY5":"Friday"
}
```

2 Save the JSON document in the "htdocs" folder of a web server – so it will be accessible over the network

3 Begin a script with an asynchronous HTTP request by creating a promise that must be resolved by grabbing data
```
fetch( 'http://localhost/weekdays.json' )
  .then( response => response.json( ) )
  .then( data => list( data ) )
  .catch( err => console.log( err ) )
```

fetch.html

4 Now, create the function to print out the data
```
function list( data ) {
  const values = Object.values( data )
  let i = 0
  while( i < values.length ) { console.log( values[ i ] ) ; i++ }
}
```

5 Save the HTML document alongside the JSON document, then open the web page via HTTP and launch the Console in Developer Tools to see the data

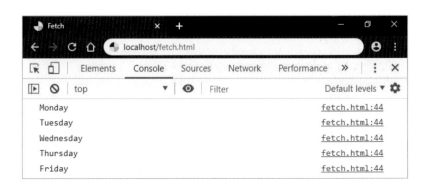

Create Interface

The rest of this chapter demonstrates the creation of a web-based app that allows data on a web page to be dynamically updated without reloading the page. The interface provides an input form and a table with a number of empty cells. Some table cells get initially populated with JSON data, and others are computed.

webapp.html

 Create an HTML document that has a table within a division in the body section of the document

```
<div id = "databox">
<table>
<tr>
<td></td> <td class="col">1</td>
<td class="col">2</td> <td class="col">3</td>
<td class="col">4</td> <td class="col">5</td>
<td class="tot">Total</td>
</tr>

<tr>
<td class="row">1</td> <td id="n0"></td>
<td id="n1"></td> <td id="n2"></td>
<td id="n3"></td> <td id="n4"></td>
<td id="rt1" class="tot"></td>
</tr>

<tr>
<td class="row">2</td> <td id="n5"></td>
<td id="n6"></td> <td id="n7"></td>
<td id="n8"></td> <td id="n9"></td>
<td id="rt2" class="tot"></td>
</tr>

<tr>
<td class="row">3</td> <td id="n10"></td>
<td id="n11"></td> <td id="n12"></td>
<td id="n13"></td> <td id="n14"></td>
<td id="rt3" class="tot"></td>
</tr>

<tr>
<td class="tot">Total</td>
<td id="ct1" class="tot"></td>
<td id="ct2" class="tot"></td>
<td id="ct3" class="tot"></td>
<td id="ct4" class="tot"></td>
<td id="ct5" class="tot"></td>
<td id="gt" class="gto"></td>
</tr>
</table>
</div>
```

Hot tip

The empty white cells in the table body have ids n0-n14, the row total cells have ids rt1-rt3, the column total cells have ids ct1-ct3, and the grand total cell at the bottom right has the id of gt.

2 After the table division add a form containing two selection boxes, a text input field, and a button

```
<form action="#"> <fieldset id="editbox" >
<legend id="legend" >Cell Editor</legend> <div>
<select id="rownum" >
        <option selected="selected" >Row</option>
        <option>1</option> <option>2</option>
        <option>3</option> </select>
<select id="colnum" >
        <option selected="selected">Column</option>
        <option>1</option> <option>2</option>
        <option>3</option> <option>4</option>
        <option>5</option> </select>
New Value:
<input id="newval" type="text" size="5" value="" >
<input type="button" value="Update" onclick="update( )" >
</div> </fieldset> </form>
```

3 Add a style sheet in the head section of the HTML document then open the web page in your browser via HTTP to see the styles applied to the table and form

```
<style>
legend  { background: Tomato ; color: White ; }
table   { text-align: center ; }
td      { width: 50px ; height: 20px ; }
td.col  { background: LightBlue ; }
td.row  { background: LightGreen ; }
td.tot  { background: DarkOrange ; color : White ; }
td.gto  { background: Khaki ; }
#databox{ width: 360px ; padding: 5px ; margin: auto ; }
#editbox{ width : 360px ; padding : 5px ; margin: auto ;
          border: 1px solid Tomato ; color : Tomato ; }
</style>
```

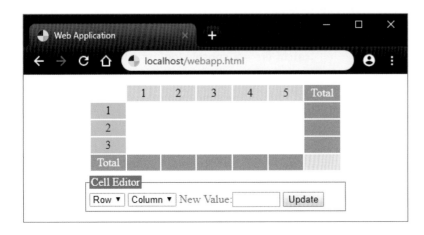

Hot tip

The JSON and HTML files in this example are located in the "htdocs" folder of a web server running on this PC, so the domain URL address in HTTP is "localhost".

Fill Cells

Having created the web application table and form on the previous page a JSON data file and JavaScript routines can be created with which to populate the table.

data.json

1 Open a plain text editor, such as Windows' Notepad app, then create a JSON document with an object containing fifteen key:value pairs

```
data.json - Notepad                                    —    □    ×
File  Edit  Format  View  Help
{
  "R1C1" : 5.00 , "R1C2" : 5.25 , "R1C3" : 5.50 , "R1C4": 5.75 , "R1C5": 6.00 ,
  "R2C1" : 9.50 , "R2C2" : 8.00 , "R2C3" : 4.25 , "R2C4": 7.50 , "R2C5": 3.75 ,
  "R3C1" : 2.25 , "R3C2" : 8.75 , "R3C3" : 4.75 , "R3C4": 5.00 , "R3C5": 9.25
}
```

2 Save the JSON document, alongside the HTML document, in the "htdocs" folder of the web server

webapp.html
(continued)

3 Add a **\<script> \</script>** element just before the closing **\</body>** tag of the HTML document

4 Next, insert a function in the **\<script>** element to perform an asynchronous HTTP request by creating a promise that must be resolved by grabbing the JSON data
fetch('http://localhost/data.json')
   .then(response => response.json( ))

5 Now, chain two more statements onto the promise that will pass the JSON data to the next chained method, or log an error message if the request cannot be resolved
   .then(cells => fill(cells))
   .catch(err => console.log(err))

6 Save the HTML document then reload the web page via HTTP and open the Console in Developer Tools to see an error message – as the function to receive the JSON data has not yet been created

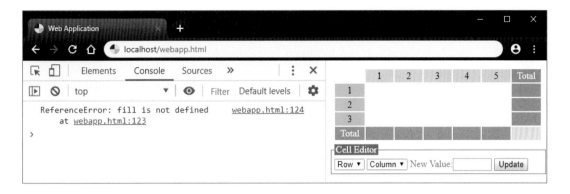

7 Return to the **<script>** element in the HTML document and create the function to receive the JSON data and have it insert all its values into the table cells

```
function fill( cells ) {

  const values = Object.values( cells )
  let i = 0

  while( i < values.length )
  {
    document.getElementById( 'n' + i ).innerText =
    values[ i ].toFixed( 2 )
    i++
  }
}
```

8 Save the HTML document again, then reload the web page via HTTP to see the values appear in the table

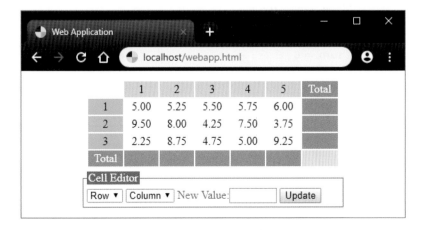

Total Values

Once the empty white table cells have been filled with data, following the steps on pages 164-165, row totals, column totals, and a grand total can be calculated and written into the table.

HTML

webapp.html
(continued)

1 At the end of the **fill(cells)** function block, just before the final **}** , insert a call to a function that will calculate the totals
total( )

2 Begin the function to calculate totals by initializing four variables
function total( ) {

```
let i = 0
let sum = 0
let rownum = 1
let colnum = 0
```

```
// Statements to be inserted here.
```

```
}
```

3 After the variables in the function block, insert a loop to write the total of each row in the cell at the end of each row
for (i = 0 ; i < 15 ; i++)
```
{
  sum +=
  parseFloat( document.getElementById( 'n' + i ).innerText )

  if ( ( i + 1 ) % 5 === 0 )
  {
    document.getElementById( 'rt' + rownum ).innerText =
    sum.toFixed( 2 )

    rownum++
    sum = 0
  }
}
```

Hot tip

This loop selects the row cells by appending the incrementing index number to the letter "n" to select the element **id** values **n0**, **n1**, **n2**, **n3**, **n4** then the next row cells.

4 Next, in the function block, insert a loop to write the total of each column in the cell at the bottom of each column

```
while ( colnum !== 5 )
{

  for ( i = 0 ; i < 15 ; i++ )
  {
   if ( i % 5 === 0 ) sum += parseFloat(
   document.getElementById( 'n' + ( i + colnum ) ).innerText )
  }

  colnum++
  document.getElementById( 'ct' + colnum ).innerText =
  sum.toFixed( 2 )

  sum = 0
}
```

Hot tip

The loop selects the column cells by appending the incrementing index number plus the incrementing column number to the letter "n" to select the element **id** values **n0**, **n5**, **n10**, then the next column cells.

5 Now, in the function block, insert a loop to write the grand total of all white cells in the cell at the bottom-right corner of the table

```
for ( i = 0 ; i < 15 ; i++ )
{
  sum +=
  parseFloat( document.getElementById( 'n' + i  ).innerText )
}
document.getElementById( 'gt' ).innerText = sum.toFixed( 2 )
```

6 Save the changes and reload the web page via HTTP to see the totals get written in the table

Hot tip

Notice that the **toFixed(2)** method ensures the cell values will appear with two decimal places.

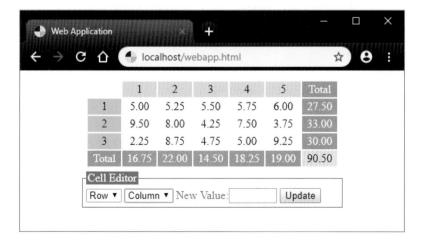

	1	2	3	4	5	Total
1	5.00	5.25	5.50	5.75	6.00	27.50
2	9.50	8.00	4.25	7.50	3.75	33.00
3	2.25	8.75	4.75	5.00	9.25	30.00
Total	16.75	22.00	14.50	18.25	19.00	90.50

Cell Editor

Row ▼ | Column ▼ | New Value: [ ] | Update

Update App

Once the total cells have been filled, following the steps on pages 166-167, the form button's event-handler function, which allows the user to update the table, can be added to the script.

HTML

webapp.html
(continued)

Don't forget

The **parseFloat( )** function must be used here to convert the String text input into a Number data type for arithmetic to be performed by the script.

1 Begin a function that initializes six variables
```
function update( ) {

    let row =
    document.getElementById( 'rownum' ).options.selectedIndex
    let col =
    document.getElementById( 'colnum' ).options.selectedIndex
    let newval =
    parseFloat( document.getElementById( 'newval' ).value )
    let legend = document.getElementById( 'legend' )
    let target = null

    // Statements to be inserted here.

}
```

2 Next, in the function block, insert statements that validate the form data and write an advisory message if it's invalid
```
if( row === 0 ) { legend.innerText = 'Select a row' ; return }
if( col === 0 ) { legend.innerText = 'Select a column' ; return }
if( !newval ) { legend.innerText = 'Enter a value' ; return }
if( isNaN( newval ) )
{ legend.innerText = 'Enter a number' ; return }
```

3 Now, in the function block, enter the user's valid input value into the chosen cell then calculate and apply the new totals
```
target = ( ( ( row - 1 ) * 5 ) + col ) -1
document.getElementById( 'n' + target ).innerText =
newval.toFixed( 2 )
total( )
```

4 Finally, in the function block, reset the form for further input
```
document.getElementById( 'rownum' ).options[ 0 ].selected =
true
document.getElementById( 'colnum' ).options[ 0 ].selected =
true
document.getElementById( 'newval' ).value = ' '
legend.innerText = 'Cell Editor'
```

5 Save the HTML document then open the web page in your browser via HTTP and edit a cell value to see the totals get updated

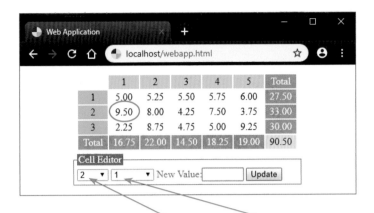

For example: Select the second row and the first column

While the entry is incomplete you can click the button to see the validation messages appear.

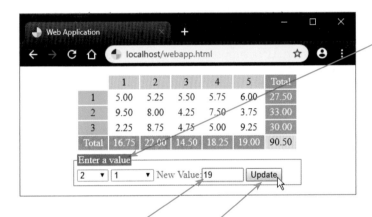

Enter a new value and click the button

The **toFixed(2)** function ensures that whole number inputs appear with two decimal places.

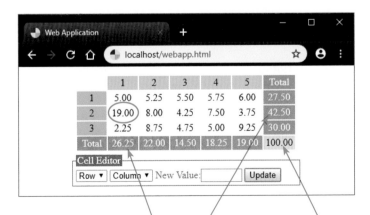

See the cell value, column total, row total, and grand total all get updated and see the form reset for further editing

Summary

- JSON is a text format that is used to store and exchange data and is a subset of the JavaScript language.

- **JSON** objects contain a comma-separated list of key:value pairs within curly brackets.

- All keys in a **JSON** object must be of the String data type.

- All values in a **JSON** object can only be of the String, Number, Object, Array, Boolean, or **null** data type.

- JavaScript objects can be converted to **JSON** objects by the **JSON.stringify( )** method.

- **JSON** objects can be converted to JavaScript objects by the **JSON.parse( )** method.

- JavaScript is a single-threaded synchronous language, but browser APIs support some asynchronous operations.

- The event loop constantly monitors the state of the call stack and callback queue.

- A **Promise** object represents the eventual completion or failure of an asynchronous operation and its resulting value.

- Methods **then( )** and **catch( )** can be chained to a **Promise** object to handle the results of an asynchronous operation.

- The Fetch API can be used in JavaScript to asynchronously grab resources over a network.

- On completion, the **fetch( )** method returns a **Promise** object that contains an **HTTPResponse** object.

- An **HTTPResponse** object has a **json( )** method that can be used to parse a **JSON** object.

- Some function definitions can be written more concisely as JavaScript **=>** arrow function expressions.

- Arrow function expressions treat the JavaScript **this** keyword differently to regular functions.

- JSON data can be used to fill table cells of a web application.

9 Produce Script Magic

Request Data

Asynchronous **J**avaScript **A**nd **X**ML ("AJAX") allows web pages to be updated by requesting data from a web server without interrupting other operations.

To use AJAX, JavaScript must first create an XMLHttpRequest object using the **new** keyword and **XMLHttpRequest( )** constructor. The actual request is specified as three arguments to this object's **open( )** method – stating the retrieval method, a URL, and a Boolean **true** value to make the request asynchronously.

The request can then be sent by calling the object's **send( )** method. Finally, an event-handler must be nominated to the XMLHttpRequest object's **onreadystatechange** property to handle the response from the web server. This can first test that the object's **readyState** property is 4 and the object's **status** property is 200 to ensure that the response is indeed complete and successful.

Text retrieved by an XMLHttpRequest object is automatically stored in its **responseText** property, but XML data is automatically stored in its **responseXML** property. The DOM represents the XML document elements as "nodes" so needs additional steps to access their content. For example, all element nodes of a particular tag name can be assigned to an array variable using the **getElementsByTagName( )** method of the **responseXML** property.

books.xml

Each element node has a **firstChild** property, which is the text node of its content. This, in turn, has a **data** property containing the actual text content. So the **firstChild.data** property of an element node reveals the text within that XML element.

 Create an XML document with 10 **<book>** elements containing inner (child) **<title>** elements

```
📄 books.xml - Notepad                                    —    □    ✕
File  Edit  Format  View  Help
<?xml version="1.0" encoding="UTF-8" ?>
<catalog>
  <book>
    <id>978-1-84078-840-2</id>
    <title>C Programming in easy steps, 5th Edition</title>
  </book>
  <book>
    <id>978-1-84078-757-3</id>
    <title>C++ Programming in easy steps, 5th Edition</title>
  </book>
```

2 Create an HTML document that includes a button element and an empty ordered list element

```
<button onclick="loadXML( )">Get Books</button>
<ol id="list"></ol>
```

xmldom.html

3 Begin a script with a function to request XML data

```
function loadXML( ) {
  const xmlhttp = new XMLHttpRequest( )
  xmlhttp.open( 'GET', 'books.xml', true )
  xmlhttp.send( )
  xmlhttp.onreadystatechange = function( ) {
    if( this.readyState == 4 && this.status == 200 )
    getData( this ) }
}
```

4 Next, add a function to handle the response and write the XML data into the page's empty list element

```
function getData( xml ) {
  const xmlDoc = xml.responseXML
  const tags = xmlDoc.getElementsByTagName( 'book' )
  let list = '', i = 0
  for ( i = 0 ; i < tags.length ; i++ ) {
  list += '<li>' +
  tags[i].getElementsByTagName( 'title' )[0].firstChild.data }
  document.getElementById( 'list' ).innerHTML = list
}
```

Hot tip

Each iteration of the loop here is getting the "book.title.data". Using CSS, the list items are given alternating background colors with a **li.nth-child(even)** selector.

5 Save the XML and HTML documents in the "htdocs" folder of a web server, then open the web page and click the button to magically request the XML data

Like HTML documents, XML documents can also be validated by the W3C's online validator tool at **validator.w3.org**

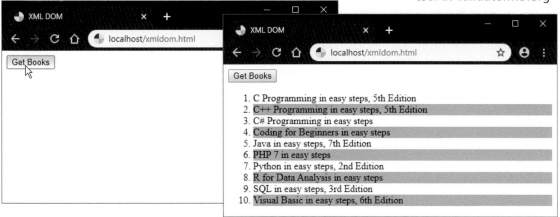

Embed Vectors

SVG graphics embedded in an HTML document maintain an SVG DOM node tree of all their elements and attributes. This is separate from the HTML DOM, but can be easily accessed through scripting to allow the HTML document to interact with the embedded SVG graphic.

The key to accessing the embedded SVG DOM is to first create a reference object to the SVG document with a **getSVGDocument( )** method. Then elements, attributes, and text in the SVG document can be addressed via the **SVGDocument** object:

banner.svg

1 Create an SVG graphic with a rectangle, circle, and text

```
<?xml version="1.0" encoding="UTF-8" ?>
<svg xmlns="http://www.w3.org/2000/svg"
  version="1.1" width="100%" height="100%"
  viewBox="0 0 500 70" preserveAspectRatio="none" >

  <rect width="100%" height="100%"
    style="fill:bisque;stroke-width:2;stroke:tomato" />
  <text id="svgTxt" x="10" y="50" font-family="sans-serif"
    font-size="30" fill="tomato">SVG Text</text>
  <circle id="svgBtn" cx="460" cy="35" r="30"
    fill="tomato" cursor="pointer" />
</svg>
```

svgdom.html

2 Next, create an HTML document that embeds the SVG graphic, and includes a text input field and a push button

```
<embed id="svgDoc" src="banner.svg"
  type ="image/svg+xml" width="500" height="70" >
<br>
<input id="htmTxt" size="50" >
<button id="htmBtn">Send To SVG Document</button>
```

Notice that this example gets initialized by the **window.onload** event.

3 Now, in a script element, create a reference to the SVG document and elements within both documents

```
function loadSVG( ) {
  const svgDoc =
  document.getElementById( 'svgDoc' ).getSVGDocument( )
  const svgTxt = svgDoc.getElementById( 'svgTxt' )
  const svgBtn = svgDoc.getElementById( 'svgBtn' )
  const htmTxt = document.getElementById( 'htmTxt' )
  const htmBtn = document.getElementById( 'htmBtn' )

  // Statements to be inserted here.
}
onload = loadSVG
```

4 Insert statements to specify a click event-handler function for the HTML push button
htmBtn.addEventListener('click', function ( ) {
  svgTxt.lastChild.replaceWith(htmTxt.value)
  htmTxt.value = ' ' })

5 Then, insert statements to specify a click event-handler function for the SVG circle
svgBtn.addEventListener('click', function ( ) {
  htmTxt.value = svgTxt.lastChild.wholeText
  svgTxt.lastChild.replaceWith('SVG Text') })

6 Save the HTML and SVG documents in the "htdocs" folder of a web server, then open the web page in your browser and enter some text – click the button and circle to see your text move magically between HTML and SVG

Notice that in the SVG DOM the actual text is contained in the **wholeText** property of the **lastChild** node of the SVG **<text>** element.

Discover more about the SVG DOM online at **w3.org/TR/SVG11/ svgdom.html**

Paint Canvas

In HTML, the **<canvas>** element creates a bitmap canvas area on the page in which JavaScript can paint shapes and text using methods and properties of the Canavas2D API. Animations can easily be created on a canvas simply by repeatedly clearing the current canvas then repainting it with shapes at a modified position faster than the human eye can detect. The fundamental components of a canvas animation script are:

● Initialize a **Context** object and shape starting positions.

● Clear the canvas, then paint shapes onto the canvas.

● Calculate new shape positions for the next repaint.

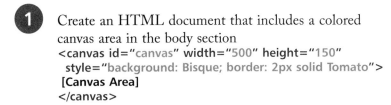

canvas.html

 1 Create an HTML document that includes a colored canvas area in the body section

```
<canvas id="canvas" width="500" height="150"
  style="background: Bisque; border: 2px solid Tomato">
[Canvas Area]
</canvas>
```

2 Next, begin a script with a function that initializes a context object property after the HTML DOM content has loaded, then initializes variables with the canvas size, X and Y coordinates for the starting position of a "ball", and its direction step size

```
function init( )  {

  const canvas = document.getElementById( 'canvas' )

  if ( canvas.getContext )
  {
    const context = canvas.getContext( '2d' )
    const cw = canvas.width
    const ch = canvas.height
    let x = 5 , y = 44 , dx = 5 , dy = 5
    context.fillStyle = 'Red'

    // Statements to be inserted here.

  }
}

document.addEventListener( 'DOMContentLoaded', init )
```

Hot tip

To paint on a canvas, the script must first create a CanvasRenderingContext2D object that has the painting methods and properties. Here, the object is assigned to the variable named **context**. Notice that the initializing function gets called when the **DOMContentLoaded** event fires.

3 Now, insert statements to calculate new X and Y coordinates and call a function to paint the ball onto the canvas every 25 milliseconds

```
setInterval( function( ) {
  if ( ( x + dx > cw-30 ) || ( x + dx < 10 ) ) dx = -dx
  if ( ( y + dy > ch-30 ) || ( y + dy < 10 ) ) dy = -dy
  x += dx
  y += dy
  paint( context, cw, ch, x, y )  } , 25 )
```

Notice how the polarity of the direction step gets reversed when the ball collides with a perimeter – so it doesn't bounce right off the canvas.

4 Finally, add the function to actually paint the ball onto the canvas

```
function paint( context, cw, ch, x, y ) {
  context.clearRect( 0, 0, cw, ch )
  context.beginPath( )
  context.arc( x, y, 30, 0, ( Math.Pi * 2 ), true )
  context.fill( )
}
```

Create static background and borders as styles – so they need not be repeatedly painted.

5 Save the HTML document and script, then open the web page in your browser to see the animated ball magically bounce around the canvas

177

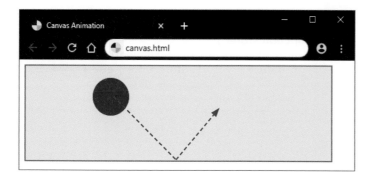

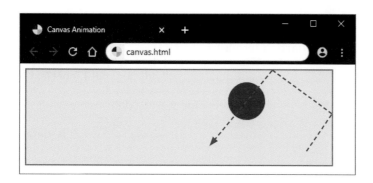

Discover more about the Canvas2D API online at **html.spec.whatwg.org/ multipage/canvas.html**

Store Data

The ability to store user data is supported by the excellent Web Storage API that makes storing user data a breeze. This provides a **localStorage** object, which retains stored data even after the browser has been closed, and the **sessionStorage** object, which retains stored data only until the browser gets closed. Each of these objects has identical methods to store and retrieve data. The **setItem( )** method requires two arguments to specify a key and the data to be stored – for example, using the key "Name" in **localStorage.setItem("Name", "Mike")**. Stored data can then be retrieved by specifying the key as the sole argument to the **getItem( )** method, or removed by specifying the key as the sole argument to a **removeItem( )** method. Additionally, all stored items can be deleted using the **clear( )** method – without any arguments.

Beware

All data in **localStorage** and **sessionStorage** is stored as string values – so adding retrieved values of 5 and 7 will get concatenated as 57.

webstorage.html

1 Create an HTML document that contains a fieldset with a text input and three buttons

```html
<fieldset> <legend id="legend" >Enter Data</legend>
<input id="data" type="text" >
<button onclick="store( )">Store Data</button>
<button onclick="recall( )">Recall Data</button>
<button onclick="remove( )">Reset</button> </fieldset>
```

2 Next, create an event-handler function for the first button – to save the data in local storage if valid

```javascript
function store( ) {
  let data = document.getElementById( 'data' ).value
  if( data === '' ) { return false } else {
    localStorage.setItem( 'ls_data' , data )
    document.getElementById( 'data' ).value = ''
    document.getElementById( 'legend' ).innerText =
    localStorage.getItem( 'ls_data' ) + ' - Is Stored' )
  }
}
```

Don't forget

Pages must be served via HTTP (from a web server) to use Web Storage. It provides an alternative to cookie storage and offers a much larger capacity of at least 5MB.

3 Next, add an event-handler function for the second button – to retrieve and display the data in local storage

```javascript
function recall( ) {
  if ( localStorage.getItem( 'ls_data' ) === null ) {
    document.getElementById( 'legend' ).innerText =
    'Enter Data' ; return false } else {
    document.getElementById( 'data' ).value = ''
    document.getElementById( 'legend' ).innerText =
    'Stored Data: ' + localStorage.getItem( 'ls_data' )
  }
}
```

4 Finally, add an event-handler function for the third button – to remove the data in local storage

```
function remove( ) {
  if ( localStorage.getItem( 'ls_data' ) === null ) {
    document.getElementById( 'legend' ).innerText =
    'Enter Data' ; return false } else {
      document.getElementById( 'legend' ).innerText =
      localStorage.getItem( 'ls_data' ) + ' Is Removed'
      localStorage.remove( 'ls_data' )
      document.getElementById( 'data' ).value = ''
  }
}
```

Hot tip

A shorthand alternative lets you simply tag the key onto the object name. For example **localStorage.setItem('A','1')** can be expressed as **localStorage.A='1'**, and **localStorage.getItem('A')** as **localStorage.A**

5 Save the HTML document in the "htdocs" folder of a web server, then open the web page in your browser, enter some text, and hit "Store Data"

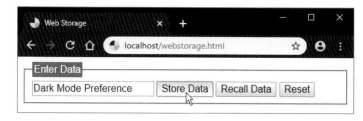

6 Restart your browser and re-open this web page, then push the "Recall Data" button to see the data has been magically retained – push "Remove Data" to delete it

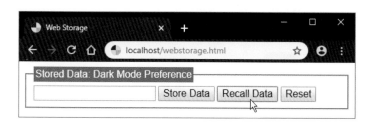

Discover more about the Web Storage API online at html.spec.whatwg.org/multipage/webstorage.html

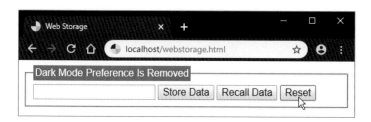

Drag Items

The ability to allow the user to drag page objects and drop them onto a target is supported by the Drag-and-Drop API. This specifies many events that fire when the user drags an object, but most important are the "dragstart", "dragover", and "drop" events. Event-handlers need to be scripted for each one of these events:

- **ondragstart event-handler** – to specify the Text data to be attached to the object being dragged when dragging starts.

- **ondragover event-handler** – to cancel the default behavior of the drop target, thereby allowing objects to be dropped on it.

- **ondrop event-handler** – to define what should happen when an object gets dropped on the drop target.

Additionally, the ondrop event-handler should typically ensure that the target cannot be dropped on itself:

dragndrop.html

1 Create an HTML document with a paragraph that contains images plus an empty list in a fieldset

```
<p>
<img id="bin" src="bin.png" alt="Bin">
<img class="folder" id="Red" src="red.png" alt="Folder">
<img class="folder" id="Yellow" src="yel.png" alt="Folder">
<img class="folder" id="Green" src="grn.png" alt="Folder">
</p>
<fieldset>
<legend>Folders Dropped:</legend>
<ol id="list" ></ol>
</fieldset>
```

Folders Dropped:

2 Begin a script with a statement to add an event listener after the DOM has completely loaded

```
document.addEventListener
            ( 'DOMContentLoaded', dragNdrop )
```

3 Next, create the event-handler function that begins by getting references to the images and list elements

```
function dragNdrop( ) {
  const bin = document.getElementById( 'bin' )
  const folders =
  document.getElementsByClassName( 'folder' )
  const list = document.getElementById( 'list' )
  // Statements to be inserted here.
}
```

4 Now, insert statements to attach event-handlers to each folder image and cancel the default behavior of the bin

```
let i = 0
for( i = 0 ; i < folders.length ; i++ ) {
  folders[ i ].ondragstart = function( event ) {
    event.dataTransfer.setData( 'Text', this.id ) }
}
bin.ondragover = function( event ) { return false }
```

Notice that the arguments to the dragstart event's **dataTransfer.setData( )** method specify the data format and the actual data – in this case the "Text" format and the **id** of the dragged element.

5 Finally, insert statements to get the **id** and element reference of the folder being dropped, then (unless it's the bin) write its **id** into the list and delete that folder image

```
bin.ondrop = function( event ) {
  const did = event.dataTransfer.getData( 'Text' )
  const tag = document.getElementById( did )
  if ( did === 'bin' ) { return false }
  else { list.innerHTML += '<li>' + did }
  tag.parentNode.removeChild( tag )
}
```

Discover more about the Drag-and-Drop API online at **html.spec. whatwg.org/multipage/ dnd.html**

6 Save the HTML document then open it in your browser and magically drag and drop folders into the bin

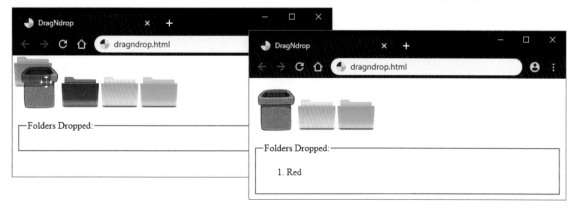

Pass Messages

The ability to allow plain text messages to be securely sent between documents is supported by the Messaging API. This is even possible when the documents are hosted on two different domains. For example, a document hosted on the local domain might include an inline frame containing a document from a different domain, which can securely send messages to each other.

To send a message to another document, a reference to the receiving document's containing window is first required by the sending document. For an inline frame this is available from its **contentWindow** property. The Messaging API then provides it a **postMessage( )** method that requires two arguments – to specify the message to be sent, and the target document domain – for example, **otherWindow.postMessage('Hello', 'http://example.com')**

In order to receive a message sent from another document, a message "listener" must first be added to the receiving document. This requires three arguments be supplied to that window's **addEventListener( )** method – to specify it should listen for a "message" type, the event-handler function to process the message, and a Boolean **false** value to indicate no further processing is required.

The message is passed to the event-handler as an "event" that has an **origin** property, containing the domain of the sending document, and a **data** property, containing the text message.

Don't forget

Pages must be served via HTTP (from a web server) to use the Messaging API. As a security precaution, cross-document messaging only succeeds when the sender correctly specifies the receiver's domain in the **postMessage( )** method, and the receiver correctly verifies the sender's domain in the message's **event.origin** property.

sender.html

1 Create an HTML document that incorporates a heading, a paragraph to display the document domain, an inline frame for a remote domain, and a "Send Message" button
<h1>Sender</h1>

<p id="host" >Main Page Domain: </p>

<iframe id="cage" width = "450" height = "120"
  src="http://example.com/receiver.html" > </iframe>

<button onclick="sendMsg( )" >Send Message</button>

2 Next, begin a script to display the domain that is hosting this HTML document
document.getElementById('host').innerText +=
document.domain

3 Now, add a function to send a message
```
function sendMsg( ) {
  const cage =
  document.getElementById( 'cage' ).contentWindow
  cage.postMessage( 'Message Received from: ' +
        document.domain , 'http://example.com' )
}
```

4 Create another HTML document that incorporates a
heading, a paragraph to display the document domain,
and an empty paragraph – in which to receive a message
```
<h1>Receiver</h1>
<p id="host" >Iframe Page Domain: </p>
<p id="msg"></p>
```

receiver.html

5 Begin a script to display the domain that is hosting this
second HTML document, and add a message event listener
```
document.getElementById( 'host' ).innerText +=
document.domain
window.addEventListener( 'message', readMsg )
```

6 Now, add a function to write a received message
```
function readMsg( event ) {
  if ( event.origin === 'http://localhost' )
  document.getElementById( 'msg' ).innerText = event.data
}
```

Discover more about the
Messaging API online
at html.spec.whatwg.
org/multipage/web-
messaging.html

7 Save the documents on different domains, then click the
button to magically send a cross-document message

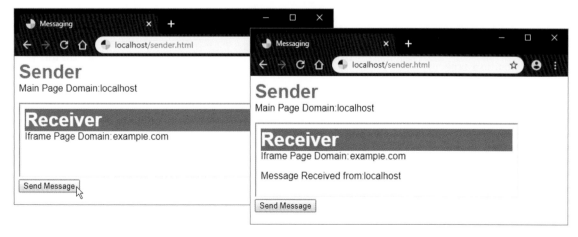

Locate Users

The ability to pinpoint the user's geographic location is supported by the wonderful Geolocation API. This first requests the user's consent to share location details – to send information about nearby wireless access points and the computer's IP address to, for example, Google Location Services. This service returns the user's estimated latitude and longitude coordinates. Coordinates successfully retrieved can be displayed on the page and supplied to the Google Maps service to acquire a map at that location:

geolocation.html

1 Create an HTML document that contains two fixed-size paragraphs in the body section

```
<p id = "msg" style = "width:450px;height:50px" ></p>
<p id = "map" style = "width:450px;height:200px"></p>
```

2 Next, add an element in the document's head section to grab the Google Maps API

```
<script src =
  "//maps.googleapis.com/maps/api/js?key=API_KEY " >
</script>
```

3 Now, begin a script at the end of the document's body section with a function that attempts to seek the user location when the HTML document has loaded

```
function init( ) {

  if ( navigator.geolocation ) {
    document.getElementById( 'msg' ).innerText =
    'Geolocation service is trying to find you...'
    navigator.geolocation.getCurrentPosition( success , fail )
  } else {
    document.getElementById( 'msg' ).innerText =
    'Your browser does not support Geolocation service'
  }
}
document.addEventListener( 'DOMContentLoaded', init )
```

Don't forget

In this example, the **navigator.geolocation** object provides the **getCurrentPosition( )** method that must specify functions to handle success and failure. These functions must each accept a returned **position** object argument, as that contains the coordinates, or error details.

4 Then, add a function to display a message if the attempt fails

```
function fail( position ) {

  document.getElementById( 'msg' ).innerText =
  'Geolocation service cannot find you at this time'
}
```

5 Finally, add a success function to display the retrieved coordinates and a map when the attempt succeeds

```
function success( position ) {

    const lat = position.coords.latitude
    const lng = position.coords.longitude
    document.getElementById( 'msg' ).innerHTML =
    'Found you at...<br>Latitude: ' + lat + ' , Longitude: ' + lng

    const latlng = new google.maps.LatLng( lat , lng )
    const options = { zoom: 18 , center : latlng ,
        mapTypeId: google.maps.MapTypeId.ROADMAP }
    const map = new google.maps.Map
        ( document.getElementById( 'map' ) , options )
    const marker = new google.maps.Marker
      ( { position: latlng , map: map , title: 'You are here' } )
}
```

Hot tip

To replicate this example you will first need to sign into the Google Cloud Platform online at **cloud.google.com** and create a new project. Then, enable the Maps JavaScript API for your project and get an API key. Replace *API_KEY* in Step 2 with your own key to run the example.

6 Save the HTML document in the "htdocs" folder of a local web server, then open the web page and allow your location to be known – to get magically pinpointed

W3C®

Discover more about the Geolocation API online at **w3.org/TR/geolocation**

185

Summary

- AJAX allows web pages to be updated by requesting data from a web server without interrupting other operations.

- A successful **XMLHttpRequest** stores text in its **responseText** property and XML data in its **responseXML** property.

- SVG graphics embedded in an HTML document maintain an SVG DOM node tree of all their elements and attributes.

- The **getSVGDocument( )** method creates a reference object of elements, attributes, and text in an SVG document.

- The Canavas2D API provides methods and properties that can paint shapes and text onto a canvas area.

- The **getContext( )** method creates a reference object of a canvas area.

- The Web Storage API provides a long term **localStorage** object and a **sessionStorage** object for temporary storage.

- Items can be stored in **localStorage** or **sessionStorage** using the **setItem( )** method to specify a key and the data.

- The Drag-and-Drop API allows the user to drag page objects and drop them onto a target.

- Event-handlers need to be scripted for dragstart, dragover, and drop events to create a drag and drop interface.

- The Messaging API allows plain text messages to be securely sent between documents – even those on different domains.

- To receive a message, the receiving document must correctly identify the domain hosting the sending document.

- The Geolocation API provides the ability to pinpoint the user's location if they consent to share location details.

- Google Location Services returns the user's estimated latitude and longitude coordinates.

- Location coordinates can be displayed on the page and supplied to Google Maps to acquire a map at that location.

Index

189